JOHNNY DEPP

JOHNNY
DEPP

The Unauthorized Biography

•

DANNY WHITE

Michael O'Mara Books Limited

First published in Great Britain in 2011 by
Michael O'Mara Books Limited
9 Lion Yard
Tremadoc Road
London SW4 7NQ

A CIP catalogue record for this book is available from the British Library.

Papers used by Michael O'Mara Books Limited are natural, recyclable products made from wood grown in sustainable forests. The manufacturing processes conform to the environmental regulations of the country of origin.

ISBN: 978-1-84317-613-8 (hardback)
ISBN: 978-1-84317-653-4 (trade paperback)

1 2 3 4 5 6 7 8 9 10

www.mombooks.com

Cover design by Ana Bjezancevic

Designed and typeset by D23

Printed in the UK by CPI William Clowes Ltd, Beccles, NR34 7TL

To LMD – a fountain of inspiration.
Sláinte!

CONTENTS

INTRODUCTION

Too many Hollywood actors are insufferably precious about their trade, attempting to elevate an admirable profession to inappropriately saintly heights. This departure from reality – so hilariously sent up by Ricky Gervais in his anchoring of the Golden Globes in 2011 – has made the public somewhat weary of them as a breed.

Johnny Depp, though arguably the finest actor of his generation and certainly the most exciting, is refreshingly honest and down to earth about his trade. 'The way I look at it is that I'm paid insane amounts of money to make different faces and tell lies, pretending to be someone else,' he said of how he earns his crust. Indeed, he even rejects the title of 'film star', arguing: 'I'm much more "in the trenches" than sort of glittery – I'm not very good at that!'

In truth, Depp is sublime in both the trenches and among the glitter. He has brilliantly tackled characters on the fringes of society, but he can play mainstream roles with just as much panache.

His pin-up looks bring glitter aplenty to the party, too. Many good-looking stars disingenuously claim that they are uncomfortable with their pin-up crown. Depp, as we shall see throughout his story, genuinely is a reluctant heart-throb. But a heart-throb he certainly is: one British tabloid described him as 'the 1990s' woman's ultimate wet dream'. As his fame has soared, he has received increasingly raunchy fan mail. Enclosed with some of the letters that pour into his office have been everything from home-made explicit videos, underwear of varying degrees of newness and even body hair.

On the set of one movie, a teenage girl approached a member of the crew and asked him how much he would charge her for access to some of Depp's excrement. 'Terrifying idea,' said the embarrassed actor when he learned of this.

Had he chosen to rely on nothing but his looks, Depp could have had an easy and profitable career. Film-makers and fashion houses would have rolled the red carpet out for him, but he always wanted to aim far higher than that. 'I don't want to make a career of taking my shirt off,' he said.

Indeed, while women across the globe swoon over him and many men secretly wish they shared Depp's handsome appearance, the man himself admits to being touchingly self-conscious when it comes to his looks. He absolutely loathes watching himself on screen. 'I am up there with my gigantic nose,' he said. 'I am a big old dog with a gigantic nose. That is how I often see myself when I watch my own movies.'

•

Depp has proved just as capable of turning down huge

earning films as he is of taking small parts in fringe flicks. He has tussled with some of the choices he has been forced to make, but always stayed essentially true to his principles. 'I'm not sure what's scarier, commercial failure or commercial success,' he once pondered. 'I think commercial success is a much more scary notion.' In recent years he has embraced the blockbuster, but for some time he was the epitome of choosiness. He reasoned that if his heavily discerning stance meant he fell out of favour altogether as an actor, then that was far from the end of the world. 'I figured I could always go back to playing guitar or pumping gas or something,' he said.

It was after he became a father that he relaxed and broadened his range. Not out of a growing desire for financial security, but for the more touching reason that he wanted to appear in films that his children would enjoy, such as *Alice in Wonderland*. As the star of the *Pirates of the Caribbean* series, which has taken nearly $3 billion at the box office, he is certainly firmly in the mainstream now. 'It doesn't feel any different than anything I've ever done,' he told *Rolling Stone* magazine of his involvement in that franchise. 'It's just that more people saw this movie and liked this character.' His interpretation of Captain Jack Sparrow is quirky and admirably eccentric.

His take on the character made Walt Disney executives

enormously nervous during the early weeks on set of the first movie, but he stood firm when they raised their concerns with him. This was to everyone's benefit as his emotive performances became pivotal to the film's appeal for the audiences. His creativity often bubbles over, and woe betide any director who attempts to make this thoughtful, sensitive man conform to a pre-determined guideline.

As such, he makes for an inspiring, as well as interesting, actor. Particularly since, during this glittering but perplexing career Depp has, like many a big-screen thespian, preferred to keep secret who he really is. Referring back to one of the jobs he took as a teenager, he said that even once he became a globally famous actor, he still felt a connection with his younger pre-fame self. 'It's just an odd thing because I still feel like I'm this seventeen-year-old gas station attendant in south Florida, and that it's other people who place this strange stigma on you. When you are in some ways a commodity, a product, people create an image that could have absolutely nothing to do with you, and they have the power to sell it and shove it down the throats of people.'

At times bedevilling in his mysteriousness, the few occasions he has let the mask slip, he has ended up wishing he had not. Even during interviews he treads with tantalizing care, and often conceals as much as he reveals.

INTRODUCTION

·

Here is the true story of Johnny Depp, the man who has been credited with 'magical powers' by a fellow actor, and his weird, wonderful life.

CHAPTER ONE:

JOHNNY THE KID

sked how he got into the world of acting, Johnny Depp's response was: 'It was really a fluke – divine intervention.' Given how successful, respected and popular he has become as an actor, his passage into the industry was certainly less fiery and determined than that of many of his contemporaries. Before he set foot in it, he had already seen more of the world than a young man of his age should have done.

It is fair to say that Johnny Depp's childhood was rather unsettled. When he looks back over his experiences and feelings during his formative years, he says: 'I felt completely and utterly confused by everything that was going on around me.' No wonder he has preferred to play characters who are outsiders. It could hardly have been otherwise considering the experiences he went through during his youth.

His early years saw his family move swiftly from home to home. 'Growing up, I had a sneaking suspicion that it is okay to be different,' he said. It is a sneaking suspicion that has served him well throughout his life. That said, on the face of it, it all seemed more conventional and wholesome. Johnny was the fourth and final child of John Depp Snr, a civil engineer, and his wife Betty Sue, who worked in a local coffee shop. His mother's demeanour at work has been described as 'earthy'. The first three children, daughters Debbie and Christie, and son Dan, came from Betty Sue's previous relationship.

The surname 'Depp' is, as the star himself claimed during an interview on *Inside the Actor's Studio*, the German word for 'idiot'. The family lived in Owensboro in Kentucky, where Native Americans have lived for thousands of years. Indeed, some of their number have attached dark, mythical properties to the area. The city rests on the southern banks of the Ohio River and the fact that it is now best known for its barbecues tells plenty about what a homely, modest neighbourhood it is.

John Christopher Depp II joined the family on 9 June 1963. He soon became known as 'Johnny', in part to differentiate him from his father. However, the family was always keen on nicknames. Dan was often called 'DP'; Depp himself had a string of informal monikers including 'Johnny Dip', and 'Dippity Do'. Even Depp's maternal grandfather, Walter, had a nickname, referred to by the family as PawPaw.

Depp was born into momentous times in America. The country was still mired in the seemingly intractable Vietnam War. President John F. Kennedy was trying to guide home civil rights legislation, to bring increased equality to the country. While many Americans were welcoming such developments with open arms, others were less pleased, indeed an African American civil rights activist was murdered by a Ku Klux Klan member just days after Depp's birth. In the same month, JFK delivered his legendary 'Ich bin ein Berliner' speech. It was this atmosphere into which the boy was born. He was not breastfed, a fact that he would later credit for his passion for alcohol and cigarettes. 'I wasn't breastfed. But then, that'd be pretty obvious, considering my smoking,' he said. 'Breast deprivation can also lead to a fondness for alcohol, to a certain extent.'

He had a memorable uncle, a religious man who Depp described as 'an old-time preacher'. Young Depp was mesmerized by his uncle's performances at the altar, and was also enthralled by the reaction of his fellow audience members. Johnny spoke later of the 'strangeness of seeing all these adults bursting into tears, running up and grabbing his feet when he'd say, "Come up and be saved!" It was an obtuse sort of image for a kid.'

As a child, Depp was far from gregarious when it came to other kids. He spoke later of the different types of kids there were at his school: 'The jocks, the smart kids and the rednecks,' he said. 'Then there were the burnouts. I was one of the burnouts. None of the girls wanted to hang out with me. I was just, you know, a kind of weed-head: a weird kid.'

It was with his grandfather, PawPaw, that Depp built the most intense of his childhood relationships. 'We were inseparable, me and PawPaw,' recalled Depp of his Cherokee Indian grandfather, who had a similar facial appearance to the one we see in Depp today.

Indeed, director John Waters was later to tell Depp that his cheekbones were the result of his Indian ancestry, and suggested Depp marry Raquel Welch, so their children would have 'the best cheekbones in America – we could sell 'em to rich yuppies.'

A less attractive family trait was one that Depp later recounted to *FHM* magazine. 'I can remember seeing my great grandmother's toenails,' he said. 'She was a full-blooded Cherokee. Her toenails were really long and curled like cashews . . . Horrible, can't even think about it. Just an awful image.' Moving aside from that horror, Depp and his grandfather went picking tobacco together in Kentucky; happy days for both in which they bonded beautifully. Building up a sweat as they worked, they felt rewarded.

A self-confessed 'weird kid', at the age of five Depp's idol was American explorer Daniel Boone, who was most famous for his exploration of Kentucky. Johnny would go on to develop some slightly more puzzling heroes in time. As to who he did not admire, John Wayne was high on that list. 'I could never stand him,' said Depp. 'He seemed such a right-wing, radical sort of guy.' Among Depp's stranger ambitions, in his early years, was one he admitted to later, but only through an embarrassed expression. 'When I was about four or five . . . I was absolutely positive that I was going to be . . . the first white Harlem Globe Trotter,' he said.

So many heroes, but his grandfather was the biggest of them.

The first tragedy in Depp's life came when PawPaw died. Depp was just seven years old. 'That was a real big thing for me,' said Depp.

It is worth pausing to consider the effect that the bereavement over his grandfather's death had on the youngster and continues to have on him into his adulthood. 'Somehow I believe that he's around,' Depp has said of his late grandfather. 'I believe in ghosts. I hope I'm a ghost someday. I think I'd have more energy. But I'm sure my PawPaw is around – guiding, watching. I have close calls sometimes. I think, Jesus Christ! How did I get out of that? I've just got a feeling that it's PawPaw.' He has later experienced what he described as supernatural incidents in hotel rooms. However, back then he had lost his best friend, albeit one who was several generations older than him. Depp did have friends his own age. It is a touching testament to how true he was to his heritage that when he played 'cowboys and Indians' with pals, he always made sure the 'Indian' was never harmed.

●

Not long after their PawPaw bereavement the family moved from Owensboro. Their destination was

Miramar, a city in southern Florida, not far from Miami. Depp would later say it was a place, 'Where nothing much happens and nothing much ever will'. When the family first arrived there they lived in motels. These were unsettled times for Depp and his family. 'We must have moved about thirty times,' he said later, though he has also reviewed the number as being closer to twenty. Either way, it was a transient childhood by any standards. 'We'd go from neighbourhood to neighbourhood, sometimes from one house to the house next door. I don't know why. My mom would get ants somehow … We were gypsies; we lived all over the place, always transient. After a while, I thought, I'm not even going to introduce myself to the other kids.' Indeed, he said, he felt like 'a total freak' among his classmates.

He recalled how so many of their belongings would be left behind each time they moved. 'Furniture, my toys, schoolwork, everything,' would be abandoned as they moved from one neighbourhood to another. For young Depp, many of these locales looked the same as each other, but each time he felt uprooted due to the possessions he had lost during the transition. Unsettling stuff for a youngster.

Amid all this upheaval, he was forced to make his own entertainment and create his own experiences. Among the memories he has of this period of his life are catching lightning bugs; sibling squabbles (particularly between Danny and Christie); the sounds of Bob Dylan being played loudly on his brother's stereo; digging tunnels in homage to his growing interest in World War II; his pleasingly paradoxical obsessions with the daredevil motorcyclist Evel Knievel and the artist Vincent Van Gogh and the odour of his mother's cooking. However, there were no traditional family meals in the household. The family tended to eat what he described as 'hillbilly food' and rarely sat around the same table. When he visited friends' houses he was taken aback to see families gather together to eat balanced and varied meals. He did not even recognize some of the dishes served up.

Indeed, he was considered a bit of an oddity by his parents from the off. 'As a boy my parents always said, I was a weird kid,' he said. 'Most of all because I always did everything twice. Honest. For instance, if I drank a glass of cola, I would put the glass down, take it in my hand again, raise it to my mouth and drink. And that did not only happen with a few things – I really repeated everything I did. I think my parents were very nervous about it.'

Although understanding of the condition was not widespread at the time, this behaviour would now be diagnosed as being akin to obsessive compulsive disorder. His parents considered seeking help for their son. This was no jokey affectation, as he later explained.

'It was something I had to do. Just like if you were walking down the street and you pass a telephone pole and you get a hundred yards and suddenly the thought hits you: I have to go back and go around that phone pole. And I would do it.'

His mother, feeling protective of her eccentric son, offered him some advice on what to do if he was picked on in class. 'She told me when I was really little: "Look. You get in a fight with somebody, and they are bigger than you, you pick the biggest fuckin' brick you can find and you lay 'em out, you just fucking knock 'em out."'

The main kind of combat that Depp was interested in was warfare, and the history of it. His special interest in World War II was a strange one, considering that it focused on a burning interest in Nazi Germany. One of his favourite television shows was *Hogan's Heroes*, a 1960s American comedy drama that was set in a Nazi prisoner-of-war camp. After watching an episode of the show he would often go straight to the garden to dig another tunnel. Once satisfied with his efforts, Depp would sit in the tunnel, the possibility of it collapsing around him merely making the experience more exciting and edgy for him.

Another eccentric interest of the young Depp was in Jack the Ripper, the nineteenth-century serial killer. During his early teens Depp devoured ten books about

Jack the Ripper, a story he would much later portray on the big screen. Amid all these unconventional interests, Depp also went through the usual teenage rites of passage, and was pained when one of his friends passed such a yardstick ahead of him. 'I remember when my friend Sal first sprouted underarm hair. We were about eleven, and I was very jealous. I still hold a grudge.'

By the time he entered his teenage years Depp was already a passionate fan of rock music. Some of the first bands he took a liking to were Kiss, Aerosmith and Alice Cooper. Young Johnny had an uncle who was in a group, and this continued to capture his nephew's imagination. 'His cousins had a gospel group and they came down and played gospel songs, and that was the first time I ever saw an electric guitar. I got obsessed with the electric guitar.' He was inspired by watching the group perform and soon convinced his mother to buy him his first instrument – an electric guitar which cost $25. During a year of self-tutoring he picked up the technique by playing along with his favourite records. 'My guitar got me through puberty, girls, life, family weirdness, growing up, everything,' he said. A friend indeed.

Depp needed help during puberty, even as he was becoming a heart-throb for those who knew him. He was so caught up with his guitar that he sometimes barely noticed the attention he was attracting from the fairer sex. 'I remember walking with him and all the girls turning their heads and looking at him,' remembered a friend. 'But, interestingly, at that time he was . . . so focused on playing guitar that that was his priority.'

In a sense Depp's indifference to his attractiveness has never left him. Though he appreciates to an extent how many women are besotted with him, he has at all times ensured that he did not rely on his looks to get by in life. He has always striven to be celebrated for more than that and in that quest he has been ever more successful.

However, his aforementioned dreams of emulating his musical idols went up in smoke on one occasion. Gene Simmons, the lead singer of Kiss, used to breathe fire on stage. Depp was mesmerized by this, and one disatrous day he and his friends attempted to copy Simmons. They attached a T-shirt to the end of a broom handle, soaked it with petrol and lit it. Then Depp put a little petrol in his mouth and blew into the T-shirt. 'Only it set my face on fire; I was running down the street with my face alight.' He had some explaining to do when he got home and his mother saw the burn marks on his face. He told her that a firework had gone off in his face and, to his surprise, she believed him. 'It was one of the dumbest things I've ever done,' he said looking back at the episode. 'Not *the* dumbest, but right up there – and I have done lots of stupid things.' Frank talk, but at least he learned his lesson.

Another time he sailed close to the edge was when he decided to visually disrespect one of his teachers. Depp found it hard to settle in schools as his family moved around so much. This was a contributory factor in a spate of bad behaviour from him during class. On one particular occasion, though, he felt he was not misbehaving but merely standing up for himself against a teacher who was unfairly picking on him. As she continually told him off Depp lost his patience. He got up and walked out of the room, but just before he left he pulled his trousers and pants down and 'mooned' at the teacher – for which he was suspended from school for two weeks. This was no isolated incident of naughtiness, though. When he looks back over his childhood and adolescence, Depp sees a string of ill-conduct. 'I experimented with drugs and I experimented with everything that little boys do – vandalism, throwing eggs at cars, breaking and entering schools and destroying a room,' he said.

However, this was just the start of his teenage rebellion. By the time Depp was fourteen years old he had lost his virginity, tried, in his own words, 'every kind of drug there was' and also begun cutting his arms. The catalyst for this early hedonistic behaviour was that, at the age of thirteen, he had formed his own rock band. They called themselves Flame and Depp proudly played the guitar for them. He found the experience

29

exciting and life-affirming. When they played together the insecurities that his unsettled upbringing brought about in him faded away. He took the band seriously enough to reinvent his image. He began to wear daring outfits, including 'crushed velvet shirts with French-cut sleeves, and, like, seersucker bell bottoms'. Some of these dandy clothing items were stolen from his mother's wardrobe. 'I dreamed of having platforms, but couldn't find any,' he said.

He enjoyed the attention that his place in Flame gave him and the release it offered from the dullness of his schooling, which he said candidly, 'bored me out of my mind – I hated it'. The band played nightclubs and found some admiring audiences. One evening after a show he had sex for the first time. The girl was a Flame fan. She was older than Depp but it was her first time too. 'He said the only thing he remembers about it is that it was over very quickly and he didn't think he'd made much of an impression, as far as performance goes,' recalled author Christopher Heard. Depp and the girl dated for a short while afterwards but the relationship petered out. His love of music and what it could bring him, though, has never died.

He had his heart broken by another girl at around this time, but in the end he felt that he had the last laugh. When he was in seventh grade he developed what he described as 'the most intense crush' on one of the most popular girls in the school. He admits that, looking back, he 'pined' for her with amazing intensity. 'Shocking – I just chewed my tongue up for her,' Depp admitted. He said they 'made out' at a party and he thought his dream was to come true. However, she ended up dropping Depp for 'the football guy'. Depp was heartbroken, but was able to smile years later when he encountered her at a nightclub and noticed that her weight had ballooned after she had given birth to four children. 'What a fitting payback for fucking breaking my heart when I was a little kid,' he said. Why take the moral high ground when you can enjoy revenge? What it lacks in chivalry it makes up for in honesty. Depp would later draw on his love of revenge to play the role of Sweeney Todd so convincingly.

Around this time, he was beginning to indulge in what would now be considered self-harming. However, as he has since explained in an interview with American magazine *Details*, he saw what he was doing as a positive rather than negative act. 'My body is a journal, in a way,' he told interviewer Chris Heath. 'It's like what sailors used to do, where every tattoo meant something, a specific time in your life where you make a mark on yourself, whether you do it to yourself with a knife or with a professional tattoo artist.' He has more than seven self-inflicted scars from those days. However, these experiences were to increase his stock later in life. As a director was to say of him in later years, 'Johnny's not a bad boy in real life, but he's had some wild moments in the past which come in handy.'

By this stage Depp looked quite the rebellious teen, complete with longer hair. His behaviour more than matched his appearance. 'I hung around with bad crowds,' he told *TV Guide* magazine. 'We used to break and enter places. We'd break into the school and destroy a room or something. I used to steal things from stores.' He was simultaneously trying a succession of drugs, though he is keen to emphasize that he was always under control. He said the reasons for his drug use were 'Peer pressure, curiosity and boredom,' adding that it was easy to come across them as Miami was awash with drugs. 'I wouldn't say I was bad or malicious, I was just curious,' he said. 'I certainly had my little experiences with drugs. Eventually, you see where that's headed and you get out.' Throughout his life Depp has been partial to hedonism at times. He has moved in and out of regular use of alcohol and other substances, mostly seeming to have such use under control.

•

It is fortunate that the teenage Depp 'got out' when he did because he was about to face an emotionally turbulent and testing time. He was turning sixteen years of age when his parents announced that they were to separate and divorce. It is believed that the news was not in itself a complete surprise, not least since his parents would regularly row, but all the same he was, of course, deeply upset by it. 'I can remember my parents fighting and us kids wondering who was going to go with whom if they got divorced,' he said. Despite, or perhaps because of, the divorce, he has long been a huge believer in the importance and power of the family, describing it as 'the most important thing in the world'. He added: 'When my parents split up was when I think I realized these are the most important people in my life and, you know, I'd die for these people. You deal with it but there's no escaping the hurt. I mean, it definitely hurts.'

His mother was particularly hurt by the break-up, too. This was her second failed marriage and the split hit her very, very hard. 'My mother was deeply hurt and sick physically and emotionally,' Johnny explained. Therefore, when the split happened he decided to move with his mother. Joining him were his brother Dan and his sister Christie. Debbie, meanwhile, moved in with their father.

Depp's choice was an understandable one. His mother was in great turmoil following the split and was much in need of his love and support. He has always been in awe of her, saying: 'She's the greatest lady in the world. Best friend, coolest thing.' A true, if unlikely, mother's boy, Depp has found many ways to express his love for his mum. Meanwhile, he supported her as best he could, and he also carried on chasing his musical dreams.

•

His next band was called The Kids, which was an ironic choice of name in a way because the longer Depp's teenage years went on the less he was behaving like a kid. He was a precocious adolescent in many ways, leaving school at sixteen, taking a job at a petrol station and moving out of his mother's house. He had been influenced and profoundly moved by reading a copy of the Beat generation classic, *On the Road* by Jack Kerouac. It was his brother Dan who lent him the book and although Depp had never been much of a reader before, as he read *On the Road* he became gripped by the rebellious sentiments the text promotes. His copy was, he said, 'a dog-eared paperback, roughed up and stained with God knows what'. The state of the copy mattered little; indeed given the subject matter Depp probably felt it lent more credibility to his literary experience.

It was an experience that changed his life, as he later outlined in a piece for *Rolling Stone* magazine: 'And so began my ascension (or descent) into the mysteries of all things considered "Outside". I had burrowed too deep into the counterculture of my brother's golden repository and, as years went by, he would turn me on to other areas of his expertise, sending me even further into the dark chasm of alternative learning.' He became more of a bookworm, and more appreciative of the arts – particularly outsider artists. 'I love the concept of *The Metamorphosis* by Franz Kafka. I'd like to become a giant cockroach. I love Van Gogh. I've always been interested in people who had mental torment, weirdos. I think everybody is pretty whacked out in their own way. I deal with my anxiety by smoking a lot of cigarettes and listening to very loud music. I like Bach, the Georgia Satellites, Led Zeppelin and Tom Waits. I like Tom Waits a lot.' This newfound passion for alternative living came in handy when, at sixteen, a friend of his was left homeless and sleeping in a car. In an act of support and solidarity, Depp left his home for a while and slept in a car too.

The sentiments became the guiding force of his life to such an extent that Depp compared the Kerouac book to 'a Koran'. He moved on and read more 'Beat' authors including Neal Cassady, Allen Ginsberg and William S. Burroughs. By devouring the pages of these authors' works, he said he had 'found the teachers and the proper motivation for my life'. So as he stood on stage with his 1956 cream Fender Telecaster electric guitar, he was a 'Kid' by name but not by nature. Instead, he was maturing into a young man for whom rebellion was not something to be left behind in one's youth but something to keep hold of the spirit of forever. As for their sound, Depp himself described it as 'Muddy Waters meets the Sex Pistols'. Here he was happy: 'There's no greater feeling than playing guitar in a band.'

Once again, Depp was quick to start dating someone he met through his involvement in the band. This time it was a young lady called Lori Anne Allison. She was the sister of the band's drummer. Like the girl to whom he lost his virginity, Lori was older than Johnny. In this case there was a five-year age gap but this did not get in the way of them developing a serious relationship. A mutual friend described Lori as 'tiny, dark, pale, beautiful and quiet – Johnny was the more outgoing of the two'.

•

Meanwhile, The Kids continued to grow in popularity. Having begun playing only cover versions live, they began to write and play their own material. People appreciated these songs and when established rock bands played in Florida several of them asked The Kids to be their support act. Depp was young but would be smuggled into the venues. 'They'd sneak me into the back and I'd play and I'd split,' he said.

Among the big names they opened for were Iggy Pop, The Pretenders, Talking Heads and The B-52s. Depp was such a big fan of Iggy Pop that he became rather over-excited and made a bit of a fool of himself in front of the star after the concert. The mixture of excitement, nerves and booze proved as potent and dangerous as ever, and Depp was soon drunk and nauseous. As he prepared 'to puke or something', he spotted his idol approaching. Iggy was, in typical flamboyant fashion, wearing just a pair of skimpy underpants and had a dog in tow. 'And for some reason,' recalled Depp, 'I started screaming and yelling at him "Fuck you!" I don't know why, because I idolized him.' Iggy approached Depp, who thought his hero was going to smack him one. Instead the rock legend was content to merely call Depp 'a little turd' and walk away. They say you should never meet your heroes as they will only disappoint you. Johnny was crushed by the experience, particularly once he sobered up. However, as we will see, later in his life he would get another chance to work with Iggy Pop.

Looking back over his teenage years, Depp is keen to emphasize that he was not 'a bad boy, or a delinquent or a rebel'. Instead he prefers to consider his teenage behaviour as that of somebody full of curiosity. 'It wasn't like I was some malicious kid who wanted to kick some old lady in the shin and run, you know. I just wanted to find what was out there.'

He is keen to talk about his upbringing, including the more outlandish and hedonistic elements of it, because, he explains, by being truthful about what he went through he can help youngsters who are going through similar experiences themselves. He is now a grown man, but he insists that some things never change, however old you get. 'There are certain elements of boyhood we can't escape,' he said. 'And farts will always be funny.' Indeed, he happily admits that he is, in many ways, an eternal teenager. 'I'm sure my brain stopped at seventeen,' he said. 'I was really happy then. I was playing in a band, reading books because I hadn't read in school and there were girls around. In a way, I'm sort of stuck here.'

•

Meanwhile, his romance with Lori Anne continued. Given his admiration for the sense of security and assurance that conventional domestic bliss can bring to a person, it is not surprising how quickly they became serious. All the same, for Depp to propose marriage before he turned twenty was a big step. 'I remember him being very excited about getting married to Lori,' said Yves Bouhadana, a guitarist with the band. 'In fact, I remember theirs as being the first serious relationship that he had, so he was madly in love with her, and ready to be married to her.' They tied the knot on 20 December 1983, with Depp having just turned twenty, his wife some five years older than him.

Not much is known of Depp's marriage and why it went wrong. The man himself has said little about it. 'It wasn't working out, so we took care of it,' was his straightforward, if unrevealing, explanation. Looking back, he has been a little more analytical but scarcely more illuminating. 'I was married when I was twenty,' he said. 'It was a strong bond with someone, but I can't necessarily say it was love.' He continued: 'Love is something that comes around once, maybe twice, if you're lucky.' He has admitted that he was, in some sense at least, rushing into marriage to attempt to 'right the wrong of my parents', whose split had so hurt him. 'I had the right intentions, but the wrong timing, and the wrong person. But I don't regret it. I had fun and I learned a lot from it.' Johnny and Lori Anne's divorce came through almost exactly two years after they had first met.

Much later, when asked whether he had ever really believed in the marriage, he said: 'I really don't know'. Depp's quest for grounded domestic bliss would continue throughout his life. 'I guess I have very traditional kinds of sensibilities about that kind of stuff,' he said. 'You know, a man and a woman sharing their life together and having a baby, whatever.' Indeed, his search and longing for such a relationship is one of the few constants in what has been an exciting and remarkable existence for the Hollywood star.

It would be an existence in which Depp attempted to stay true to the traditional spirit of the 'libertine'. Returning to that epochal moment in which he first read *On the Road*, Depp has said that through everything that has happened to him since, he has remained true to the spirit of freedom that the book instilled in him. 'So much has happened to me in the twenty years since I first sat down and took that long drag on Kerouac's masterpiece,' he wrote. 'I have been a construction labourer, a gas station attendant, a bad mechanic, a screen printer, a musician, a phone salesman, an actor and a tabloid target but there's never been a second that went by in which I deviated from the road that ol' Jack put me on, via my brother.'

The road that would take him to Hollywood next ...

CHAPTER TWO:

EARLY DAYS IN HOLLYWOOD

Soon after his split with Lori Anne, Depp's band The Kids moved to Tinseltown to give true fame one final push. A Hollywood music manager, Don Ray, had convinced them that he could make their dreams come true. However, as Depp and his band mates were soon to discover, their dreams were not to be equalled by the harsh reality. The optimism in Depp's heart as he drove to California was quickly dispelled on arrival. The band – who renamed themselves Six Gun Method – quickly lost the savings they had pooled to finance their new drive – and their hope was lost at roughly the same time.

The same route has been taken by others who subsequently found success in Hollywood. Brad Pitt, for instance, drove there as a young man with dreams of fame, only to find that the first jobs he took were less than glamorous. Pitt, later to become a good friend of Depp, worked as a chauffeur for strippers and also dressed up as a giant chicken to promote a restaurant, a job in which he faced abuse from some drunken diners who saw him as an easy target. Who could have known then that this man would eventually become one of Hollywood's most powerful, successful and wealthy figures?

Who, for that matter, would have known the same would become true for Johnny Depp? He could scarcely have believed it himself as he came crashing down to earth in Hollywood. The band did get some bookings in Los Angeles, including appearing on the same bill as Billy Idol. Such moments, though, were few and far between. Instead, Depp was forced to take some spectacularly unrewarding jobs. 'It was horrible,' he remembered. 'There were so many bands it was impossible to make any money. So we all got side jobs. We used to sell ads over the telephone – telemarketing. We got $100 a week for ripping people off. We'd tell them they'd been chosen by so-and-so . . . to receive a grandfather clock. They would order $500 worth of these fucking things and we would send them a cheap grandfather clock. It was horrible.'

There was more low-paying work for him when he sold pens over the phone. 'I attribute that job as my first training as an actor,' he said. 'You would start playing different characters over the telephone because you got bored. And you would come up with different names and different voices and stuff like that. It actually turned out to be kind of fun.'

All the same, he was ultimately relieved to drop the job and he celebrated his impending departure by telling the people he phoned that, in truth, they were better off not buying the pens. He left with a sigh of relief and some useful training as an actor under his belt.

Stranger still was his experience as a car mechanic, a job he took on despite having none of the required experience or knowledge. 'I did, yeah. It was a strange deal 'coz, I was pumping gas and my boss suddenly says "Okay, you're going into the garage and work on cars now." I said, "well, that's fine but I don't know anything about cars." And he said, "No, that's fine, just do what I tell ya." I did it.' The job seemed doomed for disaster and so it proved. 'I got fired eventually, 'coz a guy's wheel fell off,' said Depp.

Sadly, though, both his dream of wedded bliss and his dream of rock stardom seemed to be lost at this point, and to face these disappointments while in Hollywood – a place where both ambition and disappointment reign supreme – was very tough for the young man. Many people, in Depp's shoes, would have returned to their hometown with their tail between their legs. There, they might have settled for a steady but unexciting career and life. Depp, though, is an extraordinary man, so he was in no mood to give up so easily. He stuck it out and was handsomely rewarded with a fast break into the industry that Hollywood is best known for.

Depp stumbled into the movie business almost by accident. It was the actor Nicolas Cage had made his debut as a cinematic leading man in 1983 in a cult classic entitled *Valley Girl*, but his real breakthrough came later that year with his appearance in a film called *Rumblefish*, directed by his uncle, Francis Ford Coppola. It would be two more years until he next captured public attention, but by that point he had made a significant intervention into Depp's life. The pair were introduced by Lori Anne, who remained on good terms with Depp after their split. It was to prove to be a fateful introduction.

The two men were experiencing contrasting fortunes at the time: Cage was an actor on the way up in Hollywood, while Depp was a skint musician on the way down. Cage somehow noticed something that nobody had previously noticed in Depp, and suggested to him that he take up acting. A meeting was arranged between Depp and Cage's agent, Tracey Jacobs. In truth, Depp arrived with lukewarm interest: he saw acting as, at best, a means to make some money to fund his musical ambitions. Jacobs, though, was enthusiastic enough about his prospects to sign him up to her agency. 'He came in with long hair and an earring and a T-shirt with cigarettes rolled up in the sleeve,' she remembered. 'He was not what someone usually looks like when they're coming in to look for an agent, which is what was so great about him. He just wasn't into it.'

Jacobs was a fast mover and quickly sent Depp along for his first audition. Serially struggling actors will note the irony in how things continued to move swiftly for the semi-reluctant Depp. When he turned up at the audition Depp looked, by his own admission, like a 'fucking catacomb dweller'. He was about to try out in a new film by horror director Wes Craven; the project was entitled *A*

Nightmare on Elm Street. The part was that of Glen Lantz, a young football frat boy and Depp doubted he would be able to pull off the role of 'a big blond beach jock'. However, almost as soon as he entered the audition room Depp had secured the part. As Craven put it, Depp had 'a quiet charisma' that he had not seen in any of the other actors who auditioned. Indeed, Craven went further and compared the still-inexperienced young actor with one of his childhood heroes.

'He really had that sort of James Dean attraction,' said Craven. 'Just had a very powerful, yet very subtle personality.' Not bad feedback for one's first audition. Craven had allowed his young daughter to come along to the audition and she had some fellow young females in tow. All were wowed by Depp. 'They absolutely flipped,' remembered the director. 'He just had real sex appeal for women.'

Within hours of leaving the audition Depp took a call from Jacobs. 'You're an actor,' she said. He had the part of Glen Lantz and was surprised when he learned what sort of figures are banded about when it comes to fees – pleasantly surprised.

•

Still, all the money in the world could not detract from the fact that Depp was now on a steep learning curve.

Many actors only get their first movie part after years – sometimes decades – yet Depp had, in comparative terms, landed his first part overnight. 'Doing *Nightmare on Elm Street* was a trial-by-fire sort of thing,' he later admitted. 'I'd never acted before. I'd never done school plays; nothing. The fact that it was totally new to me was a tremendous challenge. I'd never done anything like this, hitting marks and saying lines and thinking about why my character was doing what he was doing. It was totally the opposite of being in a rock 'n' roll band. In a band, you are four people, all working together to write great songs or to get a record deal. In acting, I found it was just me. It all depended on me and my own choices. I didn't have to answer to anyone about what I wanted to do.'

The film is set in the fictional town of Springwood, Ohio. The conceit of the plot is that if any of the teenage cast falls asleep, they will be murdered in their dreams by a monster called Freddy Krueger. That nightmare will then go on to become true in real life. Depp's character, Lantz, is the boyfriend of Nancy Thompson, the lead. He is killed by Krueger in a dramatic scene near the end of the film. He is shown lying asleep in bed, wearing sports gear as pyjamas. He is drawn down deep into the mattress by Krueger's hands, and his death is confirmed in the most spectacular style: with a huge, plentiful jet of blood shooting upwards from the bed. Indeed, it is a farcical amount of blood, far more than even several human beings could produce. It coats the ceiling and the walls, much to the horror of Lantz's mother when she comes to the room to investigate what the noise is about. Given the degree of blood, it is little wonder that many critics chose to spotlight the fact that the film was improbable in many parts.

As Depp was all too aware, he was unlikely to get much personal attention from the critics. His was, after all, a fairly minor part in the film and he was a new name, but he was still hoping that *Nightmare* would receive a positive reaction from the critics. It did. Words like 'outstanding', 'superior' and 'imaginative' were featured in the reviews. Although Depp was not named personally, several reviews were quick to offer praise to the younger members of the cast.

As for Depp, he was so keen to be able to deliver his own verdict that he undertook a bit of subterfuge to see the final film earlier than he was meant to. Prior to its release, he and a fellow cast member heard there was going to be a test screening of the film. Although cast and crew were banned from attending, the pair's curiosity got the better of them and they hatched a plan.

'Nobody affiliated with the film could go, but Depp and I heard about it and wanted to see it,' his co-star Rob Morrow explained. 'So we dressed up in the weirdest possible way. He had dorky glasses and a knit hat on and I put cotton in my mouth so my face puffed out. We walked right past all the execs who knew us.'

Although it was indeed not Depp, but the lead Freddy Krueger, played by Robert Englund, who took the plaudits and attention, the youngster had made his mark, particularly with the director, who was entranced by him. 'Johnny had an eighties, time-worn quality, and looked like he'd been around,' beamed Craven. 'He chain-smoked and had these yellow fingers. He was an older soul, somehow.'

The fact that Depp's character died on screen during the film seemed inconsequential to the actor's career at the time, but it was the first in a series of on-screen deaths for Depp's characters that would later land him on a list. At the end of December 2010 a list was published of which actors had died most often on screen. Robert De Niro topped the list, with Depp third, just behind Bruce Willis.

He received $1,500 a week for his work on *Nightmare*. 'It was amazing to me that someone wanted to pay me that much money,' he said. 'Never had I seen anything like that.' The days of telemarketing and other poorly paid work already seemed a long way away. Although he still had musical dreams, the contrast between his years of toil in the rock world and his comparative overnight success in acting was not lost on him. He had a part in what was to become a popular, iconic film that launched a franchise of sequels. (Depp made a cameo appearance in the sixth film of the series.) *Nightmare on Elm Street* opened in the autumn of 1984 and went on to gross over $25 million.

He was amazed how quickly he had landed on his feet. All the same, he found auditioning for other roles a far tougher proposition than he had expected. 'It was real depressing,' he said of the ordeal of trying out for new parts. 'Like, you know, I just thought "well, I'm just a bad actor – you know – that's it".'

Intoxicated by the riches in acting and the ease with which he had arrived in that industry, he worked hard. He studied acting methods, particularly that of Stanislavski. This form of method acting has been followed by some of the twentieth and twenty-first centuries' leading actors from Marilyn Monroe and James Dean to Dustin Hoffman and Al Pacino. Among the institutions where Depp honed his talent was Loft Studio, in Los Angeles. Again, Nicholas Cage was instrumental in his decision, as it was he who suggested Depp study there.

All the while, Depp tried for new parts. 'I just kept working and I did a few more things here and there,' he said. It was more than just a few. Indeed, given that he is now renowned and respected for how careful and selective he is in choosing roles, back in the mid-1980s Depp was far less fussy. He found he was unable to hop straight from one big movie to another, and his next part came in a ten-minute student film, *Dummies*, directed by Laurie Frank, a student at the American Film Institute. In the short film he played opposite Sherilyn Fenn, who would later find fame in the television show *Twin Peaks* and playing the lead in *Liz: The Elizabeth Taylor Story*. However, when they met her experience was at a similar level to that of Depp.

Sherilyn and Johnny were playing lovers in the film, and were soon to become so off-set as well. 'Their eyes locked and that was it,' remembered Frank of the pair's behaviour during the three-day shoot. 'But the minute we finished shooting, she had this red Corvette and they would get into the Corvette, and the windows would steam up and we would see this Corvette rocking away and then they wouldn't come out again until it was time to do the next shot. They really fell madly in love.' At twenty-two, Depp was five years older than Fenn but they clicked and were soon virtually inseparable. He and Fenn lived together and shared the experience of seeking new acting roles. Both were flush with ambition, but Depp was, ultimately, to taste further success quicker than Sherilyn – a fact that caused inevitable tensions and difficulties between them.

However, at the time Johnny still dreamed primarily of musical, not acting, success. 'I made some shitty movies when I was first starting out, but I'm not embarrassed by them,' he said. 'Especially as I didn't think I was going to be an actor. I was trying to make some money – I was still a musician.'

One of the 'shitty movies' he is alluding to was *Private Resort*, the third teenage comedy sex romp in a series of films, all which contained the word 'Private' in the title. The publicity surrounding the movie may have promised it would provide 'the wildest party of your life', but Depp was far from wild with enthusiasm for it. 'It was a stupid film,' he said of it. 'It was a teen kind of exploitation, tits and ass and basic filthiness. What the fuck did I care? I had no aspirations.' The film followed the exploits of two teenage lads (the other was played by Rob Morrow) as they spent a weekend chasing attractive women around Miami. A critical and commercial disaster, perhaps the most enduring and significant aspect of the film was Depp's nude scene. Such a scene would not be on offer so readily (nor so cheaply) for long.

•

Next up came a part in a television movie called *Slow Burn*. Here, Depp took only a minor part, playing the son of a millionaire. The focus of the film was the millionaire's quest, via a private detective, to find his ex-wife and son. It was a low-budget, poor effort which

Depp took no lasting pride in. Again, to him it was enough to earn him some money while he continued to chase musical stardom. Ultimately, though, he found himself more and more inclined to travel down the acting path, rather than the musical one. His reasoning was sound enough. 'Well, I have no band,' he concluded, 'and I've had some pretty good luck with [acting], so why don't I . . . give it a shot?' Why not, indeed?

However, deciding to focus on acting was not the same thing as succeeding in that route. He soon realized that he had struck very lucky with his quickly secured part in *A Nightmare on Elm Street*. He was not to receive another offer of such quality so quickly, however much he and his agent wished and worked for it. Instead, he faced an experience familiar to many actors: waiting in vain for the phone to ring. It can be a demoralizing experience. 'People weren't exactly banging my door down with scripts,' was how he put it.

This was a period of immense uncertainty for Depp. His divorce from Lori Anne was close to completion, but he was not sure what was to come next for him – personally or professionally. In January 1986 he was close to giving up the acting dream when, as fate would have it, he got just what he'd been hoping for – an offer for a part in a film that stood a serious chance of commercial and critical success.

His agent Tracey Jacobs called and asked if he would

like to try out for a part in a major film that was to be made about the Vietnam War. Written and directed by the highly respected Oliver Stone, who had served as an infantryman in that conflict, *Platoon* was to be a million miles away from the sort of television movies in which Depp had recently been involved. He was interested: all the more so when the script arrived in the post. Jacobs arranged for Depp to meet Stone and the director was quickly impressed by the young actor. (Depp's memory of the encounter is that Stone 'scared the shit out of' him.)

Depp was duly offered the part of Lerner in *Platoon* – a major coup for the actor. Stone was one of the most respected men in the film industry so a nod from him was just the sort of confidence-booster Depp needed after those frustrating months of inertia, punctuated only occasionally by television movie parts that he found almost degrading. With a part in *Platoon* he felt he really had arrived.

He was excited as he boarded a plane bound for the Philippines where he and the rest of the thirty-strong cast were to undertake a fortnight of intensive training deep in the jungle. The training was mercilessly led by a genuine veteran of the Vietnam War, Dale Dye. Working on a principle that a man can only 'portray the rigours of the jungle combat by getting a taste of it', Dye led the cast through a training schedule that kicked off with a sixty-mile jungle hike, and moved on to instructions in how to handle weaponry, sleeping in foxholes and eating basic, often unidentifiable food. The only respite from the military style drills were classes from Stone himself, who offered a masterclass in acting that was nothing less than intense itself. It all added up to a testing time.

'I gotta tell you, man, it was highly emotional,' Depp told journalists later. 'You put thirty guys in the jungle and leave them there to stay together for two weeks – just like a real platoon – and you build a real tightness. It's almost like a family. We became a military unit, a platoon.'

As the training moved into production proper, Depp became emotionally as well as physically tested. He increasingly missed Fenn. To comfort himself he wrote her name on his character's helmet. It was a tough set with members of the crew fighting, several being given their marching orders, snake bites and extreme weather conditions. No wonder Depp felt homesick, all the more so as a tropical virus swept through the cast and crew a few weeks before the wrap date. Depp's experiences during the making of *Platoon* must have felt like method acting gone mad.

The final film was a triumphant success, though Depp was disappointed to find that many of his scenes had been cut. The multi-award-winning film received plentiful praise from the critics, many of whom kept specific praise for the younger members of the cast.

Working with Oliver Stone had been an experience in so many ways for Depp – and he was set to work with him again in *Wonderland Avenue*, another Stone movie that was inspired by real life experiences. Where *Platoon* had been inspired by his own time in Vietnam, this film was based on the experiences of the man who managed the rock band, The Doors. However, Depp was not to be involved in the film in the end.

He did, though, re-enter the rock world in the wake of *Platoon*. No new parts were coming his way so he joined forces with an extravagantly presented glam rock band called Rock City Angels. The band – originally known as The Abusers – had formed in Florida. Once in Los Angeles they renamed themselves Rock City Angels and then their guitarist quit, opening up a vacancy which Depp happily filled. On stage with them, Depp could live his dream of being a member of the Rolling Stones. On the Los Angeles rock circuit they built up a solid following.

Were it not for a television part offered to Depp in the winter of 1986, he might have remained in the band and opted for a life of music. However, another exciting call from his agent was to see him part ways with the band. Soon after he left, Rock City Angels were signed to Geffen Records – the label that had recently made

Guns N' Roses such a successful cash cow – in a deal worth millions of dollars.

It had not been an easy decision to leave the band and as he watched his former bandmates snapped up by a hip label, Depp doubted whether it had been the correct decision. 'It was like, oh Christ,' he recalled of his reaction. 'All I wanted since I was twelve years old was to go on the road.' His decision has since been vindicated, but all the same, Depp did not entirely give up on his musical dreams. 'It wasn't like I ever kissed the guitar goodbye,' he explained, 'but I seemed to be having more steam with acting.'

A series of events in his life contributed to Depp's decision to concentrate on acting. His disappointment on learning how many of his scenes had been cut from *Platoon* was immense. He was short of money, facing mounting debts and had been forced to move in with a friend after being thrown out of his Los Angeles flat. So he became increasingly receptive to any prospect of making some money. One idea that did not initially appeal was reading for a part in a new television crime drama series called *Jump Street Chapel*, in which he would play the part of a young policeman investigating teenage crimes.

Depp rejected the offer when it first came. He felt that, having appeared in *Platoon*, he was deserving of more serious roles than this one. Furthermore, he was mindful that a part in a drama series might be a long-running affair, which could close his options for some time if he became tied to a long-term contract. 'It wasn't that I was snubbing television or anything,' he insisted, 'but I wasn't ready for that kind of commitment.' So he said 'thanks but no thanks' and passed. The part was given to someone else and that might well have been that. However, less than a month into filming that actor walked out on the show. So the producers decided to give Depp (their original choice for the part) one more go. This time, with his financial situation worsening all the time, he agreed to meet them.

His reasoning was sound and simple. 'People weren't banging my door down with scripts,' he later explained of his about-turn, 'and the pilot was very good, had a lot of strong possibilities. Plus, the average life of a TV series is not a long one, you know?' He laughed. 'So I decided to do it.'

Once more, when he met the producers he quickly blew them away. 'He was laid back, he had this presence,' remembered one of the producers, Steve Beers. 'When I first saw Johnny,' added producer Joan Carson, 'he had a felt hat pulled down and these deep brown eyes peering out, with a coat that went to the floor. He was cute as a bug's ear, but he looked like a waif. And I think that is part of his appeal: he can be waiflike, but his charisma comes through.' They offered him the role and Depp accepted it, meaning he would have to leave the band, which went on to receive its multi-million-dollar deal just months later.

In the short-term Depp felt he had made a bad mistake, but history has more than vindicated his decision. After all, Rock City Angels were not to enjoy long-lasting success but Depp has not done badly at all in the acting game.

•

The title of the television series in question was soon changed from *Jump Street Chapel* to *21 Jump Street*. However, for Depp the biggest change to result from his involvement in the show was his move from actor to pin-up. Depp was, from the start, a reluctant teen idol; he never felt comfortable with being marketed for how he looks, rather than what he does. In his early twenties Depp was becoming more handsome and desirable by the month. This was not lost on those marketing the show, and he was asked to undertake all manner of promotional and merchandising activities that he was less than comfortable with.

In the meantime, he had filming to take part in. The shooting took place in Vancouver, Canada. Mindful of how homesick he felt while shooting *Platoon*, Depp attempted to take his loved ones with him this time.

His mother and stepfather were able to accompany him, but Fenn felt unable to do so. Despite the presence of his parents, for a while Sherilyn's absence was an uncomfortable reminder of his childhood, moving from home to home in Florida. 'To this day, I hate it when I have to move from location to location,' he said, looking back at his unsettled childhood and how it has cast a shadow over his life, long into adulthood.

Depp was taken by surprise by the success of *21 Jump Street*, and inevitably its success led to more episodes. 'To be honest, I took *Jump Street* because I thought it would only last a year,' he told *Rolling Stone* magazine. 'I liked the pilot, and I wanted to work with Frederic Forrest [who was in the original cast], so I said yes.'

Having become more involved in the show, however, he quickly became unsettled by the experience. Later, with the benefit of hindsight and increased experience, he could pinpoint why. 'Television is a little frustrating for me,' he would realize. 'There's no time for preparation. In features, you have loads of time to do the work. And the work is the most important thing of all. I think that in the beginning of an acting career, everybody wants to achieve notoriety or stardom. In the beginning, that was very glamorous to me.' As with many other things in Depp's career and life, that too would change.

His fame grew correspondingly with the success of the show, but he always remained a decent and friendly guy to the crew. This was something that was not taken for granted by anyone involved. 'Historically, when a show becomes really popular, actors turn into giant assholes, but not Johnny,' said Patrick Hasburgh, creator of *Jump Street*. 'He once lit his underwear on fire in the middle of the set, but that was because no one had cleaned up his motor home in a long time. The show's success may prevent Johnny from taking features offers, but he's being cool about it, cooler than I'd be in his shoes. And if I were his age and looked like he does, I'd be dead by now. Girls follow him everywhere, screaming.'

All the same, Depp was under no illusions as to how he might be perceived. 'People usually think that if you're an actor and you're twenty-four and you look a certain way that you're an asshole. So they treat you like an asshole at first. Then they realize that you're a human being and a nice guy.' This was confirmed by one of the crew who described Depp as 'one of the nicest people I've ever worked with'.

His fellow cast members were also brimful of admiration for the rising star. 'The coolest person I know,' said Holly Robinson, who played Officer Judy Hoffs in the show. 'He's naturally cool. Everybody else tries to be cool, but Johnny just is.' His reputation for coolness seemed to have captured the imagination of one of the crew too. 'If this were the fifties, he'd move to Paris or hang out with Jack Kerouac,' ventured

Patrick Hasburgh. However, instead of taking that 'Beat poet' route, Depp was – whether he liked it or not – becoming more of a teen idol. He made for a strange member of this breed, as *TV Guide* magazine noted in 1988. 'He is . . . one of the stranger sights in Vancouver, consistently wearing the same eccentric outfit: tattered blue jeans with a hole in the knee, combat boots, a beat-up leather jacket, a weird white rag (actually a first aid sling) wrapped around his forehead and several tarnished earrings,' noted the interviewer Elaine Warren.

Soon, the whole 'teenage' thing became a weight around Depp's neck. So much so that his representative discouraged the press from going down that route. 'I hope this isn't going to be about that teen-idol bullshit,' Depp's agent warned *Rolling Stone* magazine ahead of an interview in the 1990s. 'We're really sick of that shit.' On another occasion he recalled with a shudder the day he was watching television in a hotel room when an advertisement based around him came on screen. 'This awful, slow motion montage of me. I was scared to death,' he said of the commercial, which he had no memory of filming.

In light of all this, he was to become increasingly choosy when it came to considering offers in the future – and few modern-day actors have shown such effort in taking only the right parts. 'It's easy to make a million bucks in this business doing stuff that would exploit the piss out of you,' he said. 'It's like fast food. Get in frame, get the product out there, and sell it quick.' The horror of these times stayed with him for a while. 'I was somebody else's product,' he later added, in an interview with Charlie Rose. 'And they shoved me down the throats of America and it was a very uncomfortable situation. And I swore to myself that when I got off that show I would do what I wanted, the way I wanted to do it. And I stick to that.'

In the meantime, however, Johnny endeavoured to make good from the situation. On one occasion he appeared at a Chicago youth concert, dedicated to promoting an anti-drugs message. The compère whipped the audience into a frenzy as he introduced Depp, who took to the stage to chants of 'Johnny! Johnny! Johnny!' The hysteria was astonishing and secretly Depp was shocked, but he made sure to not show it. 'Hello, I'm Johnny Depp,' he said, to the delight and applause of the audience. 'My basic message is simple: Protect your mind. Protect your heart. And take care of yourself.'

The excitement generated by his appearance was huge. When he and other cast members attended an autograph-signing session they nearly brought Chicago's public transport system to a standstill, such were the numbers of excitable young females attempting to get the chance of a few seconds' face time with their pin-up idol.

The fan mail he received showed the extent of the excitement his part in *21 Jump Street* had generated. Many of the letters were addressed not directly to him, but to his character. Some of them were so hysterical in tone that their author would include threats to kill herself if Depp did not reply. He said, to his credit, that he always replied. However, the responsibility must have weighed heavy on this unlikely, almost unwilling, role model. 'I just wanted to make it very clear that I'm not out there saving someone's life just because I'm Johnny Depp,' he says. 'That's not how it goes in real life. In real life, I won't be sitting next to the world solving its problems. People forget that this is a show and I'm just an actor. So instead of me being the cure I wanted to show people how to handle their own problems.'

Depp's growing sense of responsibility was noted by those who worked with him, too. 'You have to understand what it's like for 10,000 or 25,000 people to yell your name. Think about it for a minute. Then think of what it is like for Johnny Depp,' said his producer, Bill Nuss. 'I think it scares him sometimes. But I think he senses a responsibility to these people. He doesn't want to appear irresponsible.'

Depp found many opportunities to promote a positive message from the success of the show, its success and the influence he had acquired from it. 'The great thing about doing the show is the responses we get from people from the public service announcements we do,' he said. 'We try to broadcast 1-800 service numbers on specific subjects, but if it's a light show, there's no sense in running one. And the response to the public service announcements has been great. For instance, we did a show about a kid who had a problem with drugs. After we ran a drug-abuse hotline number, the number of calls they received shot right up!'

While he was eminently happy for the show to have this level of educational influence, he was less comfortable with the idea that an actor – and particularly he – should have a similar role. 'Things are pretty bad if kids have to write to an actor for advice. I couldn't tell anyone what to do,' he said. 'I don't want to be the Messiah or some spokesman for "Just Say No" to drugs … If I can help people by saying, "I've done this and it really feels bad after a while. I wouldn't do it if I were you," that's great. But also, the (producers) were trying to make me out to be this, like, perfectly baked cake. I don't want to be what these people created.'

●

Whether he was a perfectly baked cake or not, the fact remained that he was in a position of influence. Many stars who have found themselves the spokesperson for a generation have mourned that role. Indeed, it could be argued that the only worthy recipient of such stature is, by definition, one who is less than keen on holding it.

Depp bravely soldiered on, trying to give as balanced advice as possible. He wanted to help young people build a meaningful existence for themselves, but did not want to be pious or hypocritical. In this quest he did well. 'My advice would be to stay in school, because I didn't and it was kind of a mistake,' he said, in a typically measured statement. 'It was a stupid thing to do, dropping out. So my advice would be to learn as much as you can, and when you get out of school, continue to learn as much as you can. Just try and always do the right thing. Follow your instincts. Learn, make mistakes, and learn even more from your mistakes.'

As we saw, during his childhood Johnny had at times been gripped by a mild disorder that made him feel compelled to do things twice. On occasion, he also used to make strange noises, much to the worry of his parents. This latter behaviour – a close relative to Tourette's, a syndrome Depp has spoken admiringly of – seemed to return to him during his time of mixed emotions making *21 Jump Street*. One day he was in the fully booked first-class section of a plane, on route to more filming in Vancouver, when he became gripped by a strange, irresistible urge to shout something very specific. Try as he might, he could not stop himself from doing so. Finally, he let go and screamed, 'I fuck animals!' There was, as one can imagine, an uneasy silence among his fellow passengers.

It was broken when a man sitting nearby politely asked: 'What kind?'

Although he sometimes felt trapped by *21 Jump Street*, and the marketing of the show, he soon saw the light at the end of the tunnel. He continued to receive new offers of work, including scripts, and Depp paid particular attention to them because he was so keen for a way out of *21 Jump Street*. However, as his agent explained to him, many of the new offers of work were ones that relied on his continuing to play the game with his teen idol status. It was a frustrating state of affairs, but then one day a part that suited Depp came through the post. It was from director John Waters.

Born in 1946, Waters began to make a name in film-making in the 1970s, with a range of spiky cult films, including *Desperate Living*. Waters was just the sort of man Depp wanted to work with. Here, he believed, was a director who could offer him a new direction for his career, so when he found out that the film Waters was proposing would actually be a cheeky satire on the concept of the teenage pin-up, Johnny was excited. Not least because it coincided with a new marketing campaign from the makers of *21 Jump Street*, one that

Depp was very uncomfortable with.

When he met Waters it was, almost, love at first sight. In a later magazine interview, in which Depp was asked whether he was gay, he denied being gay, but added: 'However, if I were a homosexual, I'm sure I could fall in love with John Waters in about a half a second because he is one of the funniest, most charming, intelligent people that I've ever known. He's really a prime catch.'

Later on, Depp would face puzzling accusations of being anti-gay. Waters was quick to exonerate the actor of these charges. He pointed out that he had personally seen Depp approached and kissed by a male stranger, and detected no sense of discomfort in him. 'Johnny is the least homophobic hetero boy I have ever met,' Waters said. Depp was quick to insist that, for him, Waters's homosexuality was a non-issue. 'I never thought of him in such labelled terms,' he said. 'I'd notice the fact that I was working with a Swedish director much more than if someone was gay.'

Johnny also insisted that he could empathize with the experiences homosexuals had in life, as he could similarly relate to anyone who was outside 'the norm'. 'We all have our fears about being different,' he said, 'whether you're gay and you're afraid to come out or you just feel like you don't fit in any place in society.' However, he says he is surprised by any gay man who does not quickly 'come out' to those closest to him, adding that he would come out 'right away' were he gay. 'Why sit and be miserable?' he asked. 'I have friends who have known they were gay since they were ten years old, and they haven't told their parents yet. It blows my mind that they can't tell the people who brought them into this world something so important about themselves.'

The part John Waters was offering was of Wade 'Cry Baby' Walker in the film *Cry Baby*. He loved the fact that the film would give him a chance to mock the teen-idol trend, not least because the latest marketing campaign for *21 Jump Street* had tested his patience. 'It was such a shock to me to see it,' said Depp of the campaign. 'If I had had control over that and the posters and the amount of merchandising, I would have put the kibosh on it a long time ago. But unfortunately, when you're starting out and they have product to sell, they shove you down America's throat, basically. It's pretty ugly. So to be able to make fun of all that under John Waters' wing was important to me.'

He was still involved with *21 Jump Street*, but Depp felt able to have fun on *Cry Baby*, a parody of the teen musical that revolves around a group of young delinquents called the Drapes, and their life in 1950s Baltimore. Depp's character, 'Cry Baby' Walker, was a member of the Drapes who falls in love with one of the town's other gangs, the Squares. Add drugs to the mix and the recipe is there for excitement and tension as the 'good girl' of the area falls for the 'bad boy'. Along the way much fun is poked at the mainstream teenage culture of the time.

The film was shot in the early months of 1989, and Depp found it a breath of fresh air. 'I felt fortunate not having to pose with a revolver in my hand and kiss a girl wearing Lycra and do the same old expected leading-man stuff,' he said. 'Whenever a young actor comes out, they have to pin him with some sort of label so they call him a bad boy or that horrible word "rebel", which is so played out and stupid. This made fun of people's perceptions. It was really the only way I wanted to go.'

Waters described it more succinctly, as 'King Creole on acid'. He had always had Depp in mind for the lead role. 'The only other person who could have played it was Charles Starkweather, and he was dead,' the director added. Depp was impressed with Waters's dedication and focus from the off. 'When John Waters first wrote me and told me he was writing *Cry Baby*, he sent me a tape of *Hairspray*. I watched that and thought it was really great. But I had already seen *Pink Flamingos* and *Female Trouble*, so I expected him to be some really off-the-wall guy, to put tacks under your chair just so he can get a laugh, just for his own personal weirdness. But he's not at all what someone would think he would be.

He's really smart, and he has a very solid vision of what he wants. We got real close on the movie. He's one of my best friends.' He had been sent several scripts around this time, but the sheer irreverence of *Cry Baby* made it a must-do for Depp. 'John's was the best script around – most unique, best-written, funniest,' continued Depp, admiringly. 'It makes fun of the whole teen dilemma thing, and was such a joke on how people perceive me, or what has been shoved down their throats,' he says of his TV series. 'I wanted to work with an outlaw.'

When he decided to sign up, some of those who knew Depp were not sure if it was a wise move from him. The film would poke fun at the very teen-idol stature he had assumed: was this too soon to be sending himself up? 'There were people who thought *Cry Baby* was a bad idea,' admitted Depp. 'But I've always admired people like John Waters, who's never compromised, or Iggy Pop [the singer, also in the movie], who's been through the wringer just because he stuck to his guns. The easy way is boring to me.' For him, moving to Baltimore to shoot the film came with its own appeal. 'The big thing is crab cakes and thrift stores,' he said happily. 'So I'm pretty excited.'

Another draw was the fact that the legendary Iggy Pop was involved. 'Working with Iggy on *Cry Baby* was sort of like working with one of your childhood heroes,' he said. 'He played my step-grandfather, so it was great to have him as a father figure. One really great thing was that Iggy and I were on the same floor of the hotel, and we'd get together and play guitar all the time. He's a really smart guy.' It was a chance to make up and move on from the disagreement they had back in Los Angeles when Depp had drunkenly heckled his hero.

As for Waters, he was amused to see first-hand the reactions that Depp provoked in his teenage fans. He recounted the time that a teenage girl asked one of the film's crew if he could help her purchase some of Depp's waste matter. 'If the movie doesn't work, we can go into business,' he said.

Depp's experiences on *Cry Baby* made him all the more desperate to get away from *21 Jump Street*. In the third season he had increasing disagreements with the crew. 'The first season we hit a lot of good issues,' he said. 'The second season, the same. We dealt with AIDS, sexual molestation, child molestation, things like that. Unfortunately, Patrick [Hasburgh] left the show after the second season, and the direction seemed to change. I don't wanna bite the hand that feeds me or anything,' he added quickly, 'and the show has done a tremendous amount for me. It put me on the map. But in a lot of instances the people pushing the pens have been very irresponsible. And that's scary.'

The crew found Depp increasingly testing, but they

were gracious and savvy enough to know that merely dismissing his news was not a wise step. 'I don't always agree with him, but I see where he's coming from,' said *Jump Street* producer Joan Carson. 'He fights hard for what he believes in, and he has a tendency to fight for other people as well, which sometimes puts another strand of gray in my hair.'

His general behaviour was reportedly colourful at this stage. It was around this time that he was caught by police jay-walking in Los Angeles. As the officer booked Depp for the offence, he asked him to extinguish his cigarette. Depp refused to do so, and the officer responded by forcing the cigarette out of Depp's hand. The actor was not to be beaten easily – he simply lit a new cigarette. He was arrested and held for several hours. 'I'm not scared by those people,' said Depp of his refusal to be bowed by the officer. 'They just make me angry. You get the feeling there's nothing you can do.' He added that the only course of action to follow in such confrontations is, 'Don't take shit from them.'

On another occasion he embarked on a drinking contest with legendary hellraiser Iggy Pop in a Manhattan bar. Things got out of hand quickly, a window was broken and a passing woman was covered in glass. She sued Depp. 'There have been times when I wasn't in a good place at all; I couldn't get a grip on what was going on around me, and I'd just get tanked.

That's all right for a little while, but when it becomes a way of life, it's not good. It's really bad,' said Depp of this period. He added that it was impossible to truly escape problems of life, however intoxicated one gets. 'I never escaped, not once,' he said.

Gossip columns began to suggest that he was becoming something of a diva on the set of *21 Jump Street*. He was arrested for some alleged rowdy behaviour when he tried to gain entrance to a party in a hotel. 'He had a boner for me,' said Depp of the security guard who tried to prevent him joining the party. 'The mistake he eventually made was to put his hands on me. I pushed him back, and then we sort of wrestled around a bit, and I ended up spitting in his face.' As Richard Israels, a Vancouver attorney, explained though, the charges were dismissed. 'The learned trial judge granted him an absolute discharge,' said the attorney. 'That's the most lenient disposition available to the court and it means that Johnny is deemed in law not to be convicted of the offence, therefore he has no criminal record.'

All the same, a less pleasant image of the star *was* in danger of growing in the public mind, one that Depp was keen to dispel during a media interview. 'I have a couple of ideas where they came from,' he told the journalist of the rumours. He addressed his next remarks to the rumour-mongers themselves. 'I think that there are a couple of people, and you know who you are, who don't like the fact that I am outspoken about certain things. But, as far as temper tantrums and throwing punches at my producers, it's such bull that it's hilarious.'

In another interview he expanded on this defence. Depp felt that he had been unfairly targeted as his fame had increased. To be fair, celebrities, in recent history at least, have found that the higher their star rises, the more they become a target for trouble-makers keen to 'bag' a famous 'scalp' of some sort. 'Guys have gotten a little cocky with me sometimes,' he said. 'They either see that they can make themselves look good in front of their friends by being a man – something about their penis size, I guess – or they see free lunches in their future. So, they figure if they fxxk with you, you'll hit them and they can take you to court.'

Whatever the truth of the allegations and counter-allegations, there is no doubt that Depp was not an egomaniac. Indeed, he was undertaking charitable ventures. One such was for the American Make-A-Wish Foundation, a charity that gives a bit of hope to the seriously ill. 'It helps cancer patients or people who aren't going to live a long time,' he said. 'They write in and say "It's my dream to meet Johnny Depp", or someone, and we meet up with them. It can be heartbreaking, but you meet a lot of very sweet people. I wouldn't trade that in for the world.' He added: 'Ego, money, career – you can take it all so seriously. But faced with a kid who's dying, it all means nothing.' It was experiences such as these that helped keep Depp grounded, but in truth he has never been a personality naturally given to outrageous, diva behaviour.

He was becoming increasingly unsettled on *21 Jump Street*. However, receiving $45,000 per episode, it was understandable he had mixed feelings. 'It was a good idea initially, but I don't necessarily believe cops in schools is right or fair – I think that's a little bit fascist – but it was a great idea in terms of it helping people. It could put things in perspective not only for the kids but for their parents. They came up with some neat ideas and tackled some interesting issues. But at this point it's hard not to be repetitive. You know, what more can we do? How many more schools are in our jurisdiction? How long before we're found out? I mean, you can take artistic license to a point, but after that it becomes surreal.'

Johnny's final appearance came in the fourth season of *21 Jump Street*, broadcast in 1990. By this stage Depp had made it abundantly plain to his agent that he saw his future elsewhere. As she later said, 'He made a choice when he came out of the television series to take a left turn, as opposed to right.' He had increasing work from the movie industry, so he confidently walked away from the show. The series went on for one more season without him, but then came off the air for good.

'Coming off the show and doing features, definitely changes the films I want to do', said a relieved Depp as he left the family. 'I'm going to do everything I can – fight tooth and nail – to not be put in some teen idol category. I don't want somebody who's writing out checks to limit me, to put me in a herd of people who can only do one thing. I don't want to be limited by other people's opinions. I don't necessarily want to always play the leading man – I'd like to shave my head and sew my eyeballs shut.' He recalled with joy the day that he learned he had been released from his *21 Jump Street* contract. Cleverly, he and his agent had kept quiet when they realized that the programme makers had forgotten to renew the contract by the required date. So he was free, as he found out during a phone call he took on the set of *Edward Scissorhands*. 'My posture changed. Suddenly everything got bright. It was like Nelson Mandela, man,' he said of the South African legend, released from jail in the 1990s.

•

A significant change was afoot in Depp's personal life too: his relationship with Sherilyn Fenn came to an end. There were a number of reasons mooted by the gossipmongers. One theory suggested that Johnny was unhappy with the raunchy part Sherilyn had taken opposite Richard Tyson in the erotic thriller *Two Moon Junction*, which included full-frontal nudity and soft-core sexual scenes. The truth was that few relationships could have withstood the parties being so far apart geographically. Furthermore, both were attempting to make it in Hollywood and Depp was having notably more success in that. In the circumstances, a parting of the ways was far from surprising. A year on from the split, Fenn's career received a major boost when she landed a part in the television show *Twin Peaks*, which went on to become hugely successful worldwide.

Depp was not to stay single for long, however, and his next lover was another actress, though one better known than Fenn. Jennifer Grey first came into the public eye when she was nineteen and starred in a television commercial for the soft drink Dr Pepper. She then starred in films including *The Cotton Club*, the cult hit *Ferris Bueller's Day Off* and then appeared opposite Patrick Swayze in *Red Dawn*, the Cold War film released in 1984. She and Swayze co-starred in another film soon after, one that was to make both their names globally famous: *Dirty Dancing*.

Her star was rising on screen, and off screen she was also making waves. In 1986 she was briefly engaged to Matthew Broderick, her co-star from *Ferris Bueller's*

Day Off. That brief engagement was mirrored in her relationship with Depp, whom she met two years later. The couple had not long been an item when Depp offered her a ring and they became engaged. But in his rush to create a relationship in which the protagonists would live happily ever after, Depp had not taken enough time to check the foundations of his dream, and it was not an enormous shock when, a mere six months later, the engagement was called off and the couple split. It had been another rushed-into, long-distance affair for Depp and one that had not worked.

In later years Depp would be less concerned with privacy when it came to his love life, but at this stage he considered it dishonourable to be too public with the details. 'It's like when you're in high school, and you're going steady with someone and your friends say, "Hey man, are you seeing this girl?"' he said. 'If you love this girl, you're not going to tell your friends. I think you have to shield things, otherwise we'd all be out there cutting our arms open and showing you. Here's my blood, have a vein.'

Onstage, he had no regrets about treading his own path in search of more meaningful parts, rather than relying on the bankability of his good looks. The alternative just seemed too lazy to him. 'Given a certain amount of luck and opportunity,' he said with a shrug, 'I think anybody could do movies and continue to play the same character and make tons of money and buy a big old house in Bel Air and, like, smoke cigars and eat eggs all the time. But, you know, I'm not so much interested in that.' So, had he ever regretted, people wondered, leaving behind his musical dreams? Given that he was so keen on credibility, might it not have been wiser to carry on with his musical path, rather than moving into the acting world, where there were several trashy programmes and films for every plastic pop band that shimmered in the music world?

'I miss playing on stage,' Depp admitted with candour. 'I miss the feeling that you have, that sort of camaraderie that a band has. But I don't regret anything. I think that everything worked out the way it was supposed to. That's the only way I can look at it. If I had kept going with the music, I think things would have turned out a lot differently. Good or bad. Either way.'

•

So he chose acting, but not without reservations about the industry. Indeed, ever the self-searching, questioning man, he spoke with frankness about the acting trade and the price it can have on those who pursue it. 'I don't know why I like acting,' he said. 'Sometimes I like it, sometimes I don't. It's not like it's the greatest, most rewarding thing you can do in life. It's strange when you think about it. Most of the time you're saying somebody else's words as opposed to your own, and that's pretty weird. It doesn't make for a very stable brain and it doesn't make for a very relaxed person.'

So much for the nuts and bolts of the art itself, he was also equivocal about the industry and how people operate within it. He had quickly become wise to the sort of behaviour that keeps the wheels of Hollywood turning and hoped that observing this was not the same as joining in. 'I don't think my ideas or my principles have changed,' he claimed. 'But I've learned a lot about this business, how political it is and how people manipulate other people. It's scary, man. Power is a scary thing.'

For him to have noted these trends so early in his acting career, before he became the powerhouse that he is today, shows how strong and forceful they were. His own power was about to soar as he became a central figure in the world of movies. Soon there would be a new woman in his life, too. She was a star herself, making them, together, a formidably famous, romantic partnership.

CHAPTER THREE:

WORKING HARD, PLAYING HARD

It was in the summer of 1989 that Depp first met Winona Ryder – although 'encountered' is possibly a better word to use to describe what happened.

The setting was the Ziegfield Theater in Manhattan, the occasion was the premiere of the film *Great Balls of Fire*, a biopic about the life of rock music royalty Jerry Lee Lewis. It was in the reception area of the Ziegfield that Depp saw the film's young star, Winona Ryder, who played Lee Lewis's young bride in the movie.

Ryder was seventeen years old, very beautiful and already hot property in Hollywood. She had a string of successful appearances in film and television to her name. Meanwhile, her beauty had naturally made her a regular in the media. She was experiencing the female equivalent of the teenage hysteria that Depp had sometimes enjoyed, but mostly endured, for so long.

Born in 1971, Winona Ryder made her film debut as a fifteen-year-old in the 1986 teenage flick *Lucas*. It was with her appearance in Tim Burton's comedy horror fantasy *Beetlejuice* in 1988 that she began to truly make her name, deservedly so, given her impressive performance as a moody 'gothic' teenager. Next came a part in the darkly comic teenage cult-flick *Heathers*, in which Winona landed a leading role, in this case as a teenage killer playing opposite Christian Slater with whom she had a brief real-life relationship.

It was her part in *Great Balls of Fire* that came next

– and led to her and Depp crossing paths. He was immediately stunned by Ryder's sheer beauty. She looked sensational, wearing a revealing white mini-dress. She had only gone to the kiosk in order to grab herself a Coke: instead, she found herself a fiancé. 'It was a classic glance,' Depp later recalled. 'Like the lenses in *West Side Story* and everything else gets foggy.' They did not speak that evening but as far as Depp was concerned, the writing was on the wall. He wanted him and this younger 'Elizabeth Taylor' to become a romantic item. 'I knew right then,' he said, describing a moment of typical impulsive romance. As for Ryder, she said: 'It wasn't a long moment, but time seemed to be suspended.'

In fact it was another three months before they properly met, a liaison brought about as a result of a shared associate. Josh Richman had starred with Depp in *21 Jump Street* and then alongside Ryder in *Heathers*. It was Richman who introduced them one night in Sunset Boulevard. 'I thought maybe he would be a jerk – I don't know why,' said Ryder of her feelings ahead of their meeting that evening. Instead, as she discovered, Depp was a man with plenty of sensitivity and not a little shyness. Both qualities were ones that she found endearing. To Depp's delight, he and Ryder also had many shared cultural passions, including for musical acts such as The Replacements and Tom Waits, as well as for the novel *The Catcher in the Rye* by the reclusive J.D. Salinger.

At the end of the evening they agreed to stay in touch, and a few weeks later they had their first official date. It was at the Los Angeles house of Winona's godfather, the counter-culture icon Timothy Leary. 'Believe me, when I met Winona and we fell in love it was absolutely like nothing before,' said Depp. 'We hung out the whole day and night and we've been hanging out ever since. I love her more than anything in the whole world.' As for Ryder, she was just as excited. This was her first serious relationship. 'I never really had a boyfriend before,' she said. 'I was no veteran of relationships.' Therefore, she was keen to not rush into anything, not least because she said she had heard 'horror stories' about people who 'dived in real quick'.

However, they were soon living together and it was just months later that Depp proposed to Ryder – which was 'diving in real quick' by most people's standards. Naturally, as soon as the word came out about their relationship, the media were obsessed with the couple. Neither Depp nor Ryder was keen on publicity so there was never a huge drive for media attention from within the relationship, but Depp and his love could not prevent the press from photographing them, following them and obsessing over them. The public loved them too. Among the widespread coverage of the couple was commentary pointing out that Depp had a far more complicated back story than his fiancée. While Ryder had had little more than a brief fling with Christian Slater on her romantic curriculum vitae, Depp had many more ex-partners and two previous fiancées, too.

Depp's tendency to propose to women with whom he was involved had not gone unnoticed. Indeed, in America it became something of a cultural joke – so much so that some car owners pasted stickers on their vehicles that read, 'Honk if you've never been engaged to Johnny Depp'. This was just a bit of fun, but it showed how deeply Depp had made his mark in the public imagination. Wherever they went, they could not escape the scrutiny of the media. At one point in an attempt to hide away, they moved from California and bought a loft apartment in Manhattan, but the simple truth was that wherever they went, the media would follow.

On one memorable occasion, Depp decided that enough was enough. This would be the first time he snapped in the face of the paparazzi, but it would not be the last. Ryder recalled the story vividly. 'Johnny and I flew into LA from Tampa where we'd been working all day and we were really tired,' she began. 'We got off the plane and about fifty paparazzi people jumped out and started taking our pictures. We couldn't, like, see where we were going because the bulbs were popping. One guy stuck out his foot and tried to trip me. They were yelling at us, trying to get an interesting picture. Finally, Johnny got so mad that he turned around and flipped them off. Now, you'll see his picture in a magazine and he's going to look like some asshole.' Such attention and pressure is the price that any celebrity has to pay for fame. Such renown comes with so many rewards but the flipside of the coin is that once one has courted the media, it is impossible to cage the ferocious beast when it is not wanted.

As a solitary star, one is always going to attract attention, once one becomes entangled in a celebrity coupling, the pressure is not just doubled. Given that Ryder would not be the last celebrity with whom Depp became romantically entangled, it is important to put relationships such as this in context. Since actor Douglas Fairbanks married actress Mary Pickford in the 1920s, the media interest in celebrity pairings had slowly grown. Cheering crowds greeted the famous duo when they returned to America after their European honeymoon.

In the same decade the public was also fascinated by the tragic love of author F. Scott Fitzgerald and his novelist wife Zelda Sayre. In the following decades there were even more celebrated romances, such as those between Humphrey Bogart and Lauren Bacall, as well as Joe DiMaggio's elopement with Marilyn Monroe. However, it was Richard Burton and Elizabeth Taylor who became perhaps the first celebrity 'supercouple'. They first met on set and were quickly showing signs of great passion.

With the huge advances in technology, news gathering and dissemination, it is no surprise that the cult of celebrity has become a fundamental part of all our viewing, listening and reading lives. Although it would have been of scant consolation to them had they been aware of it, the level of media interest that Depp and Ryder provoked in the early 1990s was relatively tame when compared to the almost rapacious fascination that future famous couples would face. During the 1990s and into the twenty-first century the celebrity supercouple has become a media mainstay. Starting with the controversy surrounding the relationship of Prince Charles and Diana, Princess of Wales, then continuing with David and Victoria Beckham and Brad Pitt and Angelina Jolie – aka Brangelina – an obscene number of column inches have been filled with the latest gossip, true or otherwise.

•

However, Depp and Ryder did their best to deal with the media interest in their relationship. That relationship soon took on a professional, as well as personal, dimension when they worked together on *Edward*

Scissorhands. This development was one that Ryder approved of. 'I can't imagine anything better than to work with someone you love because then you're never separated from them,' said Winona. 'You get to go to work together and go home together – it's a real blessing.' The man in her life enjoyed it too, though he admitted to some slight misgivings initially. 'I was nervous. It's like another level of exposing yourself to someone. You know you can be together, but then to act together, be different people, especially someone like Edward . . . it was scary at first. She was nervous too. But it was great. Besides the fact that I love her and everything, she's a great actress, very giving and considerate. It was really easy working with her, because stuff automatically happens. You don't have to try. Stuff comes out.'

Directed by Tim Burton, *Edward Scissorhands* charmed sell-out audiences across the globe. A romantic fantasy story, subtitled *The story of an uncommonly gentle man*, the titular hero of the film is an artificially created man who, as his name suggests, has scissors for hands. Adopted by a suburban family, he falls in love with their daughter and, thanks to his peculiar appearance, faces all manner of suspicion and confusion.

For inspiration, Burton drew on his own childhood, growing up in California with a feeling of immense social isolation. 'I get the feeling people just got this urge to want to leave me alone for some reason, I don't know exactly why,' he said. Those tough times served him well in creating a masterful story to which outsider-types of teenage years or beyond related strongly. He also drew inspiration from classic films, including *Frankenstein*, *The Hunchback of Notre Dame* and *The Phantom of the Opera*. In the eyes of many fans, *Edward Scissorhands* richly deserves to be mentioned alongside those names.

Depp was a sound choice for the role. He could play the part with the necessary sensitivity, in part thanks to the level of isolation he felt during his own unsettled childhood and adolescence. Reportedly, though, he was not Burton's first choice for the part. It has been widely assumed that Tom Cruise would take the part, an assumption shared by Depp himself. 'I couldn't believe it,' he said of landing the role. 'The script was one of the top five things I ever read – any story, novel, anything – but I thought I had no chance. Who wouldn't want Tom Cruise in their movie? Automatic box office.'

Cruise, Depp's rival of that time, was indeed great box office. Among the films he appeared in during the 1980s were *Top Gun*, *The Color of Money*, *Cocktail*, *Rain Man* and *Born on the Fourth Of July*. Cruise, like Depp, also had pin-up looks. However it was reported that the heavy make-up involved in playing the part of *Edward Scissorhands* was more of an issue for Cruise than it was for the man who landed the role.

There were also suggestions that Cruise would have preferred the film to end on a happier note than in the script. Other names that were linked with the part included pop star Michael Jackson and William Hurt. However, the part went to Depp. This came against the odds in a sense, because prior to trying him out for the part Burton was unfamiliar with Depp and his work. Even once he looked into the actor's experience, Burton feared that he was already typecast into mainstream, pin-up type roles – the very antithesis of his unlikely hero.

However in person, Depp has the ability to blow directors away. He had done many times before – notably when he so impressed Oliver Stone when trying out for *Platoon*. On meeting Burton, Depp immediately impressed the director, primarily by how he was able to so powerfully act 'with his eyes'. Burton also felt that though Depp had traditional, heart-throb looks, he was still able effortlessly to portray an oddball character – 'and that's what I love about him'.

As for Depp, he thought that the director looked 'pale, frail-looking . . . sad-eyed', but then it was Depp on trial here, and thankfully he passed. 'Tim isn't the type to verbalize it,' Depp told *Playboy* magazine later when asked if he knew what specifically won over Burton in person, 'but in snippets of conversations he has said it had to do with my eyes ... He also felt my looks were deceptive, because I wasn't what people thought.'

Here, at last, Depp was able to break out of the mould in which he had feared his involvement in *21 Jump Street* would imprison him. He loved the script from the moment he read it, saying it made him 'weep like a newborn'. Though he realized it had major box-office potential, he felt that the story was suitably offbeat. In many ways, this was the perfect film for him at this stage in his life and career.

Part of that sense of perfection came because of – rather than despite – the challenges that came with the part. 'It wasn't similar to anything I'd played before, to put it mildly,' he laughed. 'I thought, "No way that people would see me as Edward." Then I realized that Edward was all alone, and inside of all of us is this lonely little kid,' he added. 'Edward is a total outsider. I really know how that feels. And so, then, eventually, I found him. And Edward – he just clicked.'

It was also speculated that Johnny related to the character because it chimed with his own experience of fame. *Time Out* magazine made this case, saying the character could be read as 'a gothic metaphor for the overnight celebrity that left Depp feeling like an assembly-line freak'. Burton noted that Depp was made for the part because more than most actors he could relate to being considered as something that he was not. Indeed, the more one considers the part, the more suitable and pleasing it seems for Depp to have taken on.

Depp was so excited after meeting Burton that he continued researching the part even before he heard whether or not he would land it. During those nervous weeks he was forever wondering when he would hear from Burton. 'It was now not something I merely wanted to do,' he explained, 'but something I *had* to do. Not for any ambitious, greedy, actory ... reason, but because this story had now taken residence in the middle of my heart and refused to be evicted.'

The wait seemed to go on forever; would the telephone ever ring? Depp's level of hope was sky-high, but his level of expectation was far lower. He became convinced that Burton would opt for a bigger name than him. So imagine his surprise – not to mention joy – when he finally heard that he had indeed got the part.

'I couldn't fucking believe it,' was how he later, memorably, put it. He added that as far as he was concerned, Burton had 'risked everything' by selecting him. Burton, in giving him the part, was 'head-butting the studio's wishes, hopes and dreams for a big star with established, box-office draw'.

Such was Depp's ecstasy at the news, that he credited a higher power with allowing such a development. 'I became instantly religious, positive that divine intervention had taken place. This role for me was not a career move. This role was freedom. Freedom to create, experiment, learn and exorcize something in me.' His excitement was only added to by the fact that alongside him in the movie was his fiancée, Winona Ryder. 'The fact we're in love and together certainly won't hurt the movie,' he said of her inclusion. Ryder played the part of Kim, the daughter of the family Edward moves in with. Ryder was the first person to be cast by Burton – they had worked together on *Beetlejuice* – and she performed well alongside her off-screen fiancé.

Depp became fascinated by the character and the story. Had he never become an actor, it is likely that this film would still have become his favourite of all time. '*Edward Scissorhands* is about a guy who's sort of an innocent placed into a normal – or what people think is normal – suburban life,' said Depp. 'It's the story of his dilemma and what he goes through. It's really exciting for me to be doing a movie with my fiancée, with Winona. But to be doing a movie with Tim Burton, and to be doing another movie that's not just your normal every day, shoot-'em-up, fighting, posing, kissing, gun-toting, law-officer kind of thing ... I feel very lucky.'

In preparation for the role, Depp worked hard. Mindful that a lot of the emotion that his character would generate would need to be conjured non-verbally, he watched silent films, including those of Charlie Chaplin. The film was shot in Florida, after Burton rejected the idea of shooting it in the California neighbourhood that was the scene of his own

Johnny on-set in 1985 in one
of his first movies, *Private Resort*.

His first major film role came with horror classic *A Nightmare on Elm Street*, in which he played one of the infamous Freddy Krueger's victims.

An early shot of young Johnny with Elton John in Los Angeles circa 1980.

Depp became a screen idol in the 1980s due in part to his role in the US TV series *21 Jump Street*.

Johnny married Lori Anne Allison on 24 December 1983, but their marriage was not to last. They were divorced three years later.

:en here at an anti-AIDs campaign in 988, Johnny has never shied away from mpaigning issues.

His four-year romance with Winona Ryder came under relentless media scrutiny.

His appearance as Edward
Scissorhands in 1990 marked
Johnny Depp out as a quirky
actor and was the film
that sparked his long and
ongoing association with
director Tim Burton.

In *What's Eating Gilbert Grape?* (1993), Depp played older brother to a young Leonardo DiCaprio, and love interest to Juliette Lewis.

Many felt that in his role as the eponymous film director in the biopic *Ed Wood*, also directed by Tim Burton, Depp proved himself to be a great actor.

Bad boys all? Johnny has always had the reputation of a maverick, as have his friends Shane McGowan (above left) and Keith Richards (below). But it was a shock when, in 1994, Johnny was arrested (above right) and questioned on allegations of causing serious damage in his New York hotel suite.

In 1997 Depp, seen here on set, made his directorial debut with *The Brave*.

Depp, seen here in 1995 with Paul McCartney, Noel Gallagher and Paul Weller, played guitar on Oasis's version of 'Fade Away', the first song on the *HELP* album, made in aid of young victims of the war in Bosnia.

In 1994 Johnny starred as
'the world's greatest lover',
the delusional Don Juan, in
Don Juan DeMarco.

childhood. On set, the houses in the neighbourhood were specially painted in a dull, pastel colour, and their window sizes were reduced to bring a more cramped and uptight feel to the locale. As for Depp, he would spend nearly two hours in make-up ahead of each shoot, as his complicated look was assembled. It was reported that he deliberately shed around twenty-five pounds in weight for the role, too.

The film-makers were keen to handle the release of the film carefully. To this end, they delayed revealing photographs of Depp 'in character' for as long as possible, to avoid the striking image becoming diluted in the public's imagination before the film was released. Burton was anxious to ensure that the publicity surrounding the film was on the modest side. 'We have to let it find its place,' he said. 'We want to be careful not to hype the movie out of the universe.' It opened in America in December 1990 and was an immediate box-office success, despite its release at such a competitive time of year. 'I was worried that we'd get buried by all the other Christmas week blockbusters, but the word of mouth on the movie is great,' said Depp.

The critics' verdict was mostly as positive as that of the viewing public. *Rolling Stone*'s Peter Travers made the novel but admiring conclusion that '*Edward Scissorhands* isn't perfect. It's something better: pure magic.' The *Washington Post*'s Desson Howe could barely contain his admiration for the lead: 'Depp is tender, affecting and, quite frankly, bloody pretty.'

Praise also came his way from his co-stars. In some cases they admitted to preconceptions before meeting Depp, but these were quickly dispelled when they saw him at work. 'People said he's a teen idol, I thought: "Oh, great,"' admitted Dianne Wiest, who played Avon Lady Peg Boggs, the woman who takes the outcast Edward into her family home. 'Then I met him – what a depth of talent! I'd look at him some days and I thought, he's like Chaplin – he's got a walk and a sweetness of manner, he's just an angel.' As for Burton, he felt utterly vindicated in taking the risk he had when he cast Depp. 'He's more that character than anything else he's done,' said the director. 'There's a sadness about Johnny I just respond to.'

With the film proving such a hit at the box office, there was clamour for a sequel and also attempts by other film-makers to replicate the sort of themes and atmosphere that had made *Edward Scissorhands* such a hit. Again, as he basked in the warmth of another success, Depp was keen to keep an eye on the bigger picture. 'They try for the same kind of naive, innocent character. But you have to move on. Of course, I would love to play Edward *himself* again – with Winona. But there's no talk of a sequel.'

•

In the wake of their successful co-starring, Depp and Ryder received a flurry of offers to co-star in future films. Such had been their chemistry in *Edwards Scissorhands* that other movie houses were excited at the thought of billing them together. As well as the on-screen benefits, such a paring would also be a marketer's dream. The main problem was that most of the offers were inappropriate in various ways. 'They offered us a gangster movie,' said Depp. 'I'm a mobster and Winona's my moll.'

The press had always felt it had a right to encroach on Depp and Ryder's relationship. Once they had acted together in the same film, that same media seemed to take this as a sign that their relationship was even more a public matter. As for the couple, they were more private than that. Whether realistically or not, they were certain that their relationship was nobody's business but their own. 'I don't even like discussing my relationship with Johnny with the press,' Ryder said. 'It's nobody's business. How do you explain a relationship anyway? Nobody knows anything about it, nobody, not even friends know what my relationship is like. I don't even know it. You try to figure out your own feelings and interpret them for yourself, and you have these really strong, incredible, powerful feelings. And then some writer who doesn't know you at all is writing about it. It's like, "Wait, what do you know?"'

With all that ink being used by journalists to speculate over his relationship with Ryder, Depp chose to use a bit of it himself by getting a new tattoo. He visited Sunset Strip Tattoo and requested a new ink job to commemorate his love of Ryder. It read 'Winona Forever'. Winona accompanied Depp when he had it applied; and she found it a shocking experience. 'I was pretty squeamish,' she said, explaining this was the first time she had witnessed somebody being tattooed. She was touched by his gesture, saying she was 'thrilled – wouldn't any woman be?' So much so that she found it difficult to believe that it had really happened. 'I kept thinking it was going to wash off or something, I couldn't believe it was real,' she said.

Inevitably, given Depp's list of previous serious but unsuccessful relationships, eyebrows were raised on the addition of the tattoo. Depp was all too aware that people would wonder if he was premature in declaring his love in such a permanent way. He was keen to claim a difference between this relationship and the ones that came before it. 'My previous relationships weren't as heavy as people think they were,' Depp insisted. 'But there's never been anything throughout my twenty-seven years that's comparable to the feeling I have with Winona. You can think something is the real thing, but it's different when you really feel it. The truth is very powerful. Believe me, this "Winona Forever" tattoo is not something I took lightly. Her eyes kill me.' Vivid and emotional stuff.

Given such powerful talk, it wasn't long before there was speculation about when or whether the couple would marry. 'We'll do it when we have a chunk of time and we can do it quietly with a three-month honeymoon. I've heard about places in Australia, islands where you can be dropped off, and there's nothing there at all. I guess you just run around eating coconuts, foliage and bugs,' said Johnny. At this stage Ryder, too, was expressing an interest in their tying the knot. 'I've got the feeling that this is right,' she said. 'I want to have, like, a honeymoon and the whole shebang. We're going to get married as soon as we have time and we're not working.' She admitted that they had not spent much time discussing when the marriage would be, 'But it will be,' she insisted.

So much for words; it was the actions of both parties that were of more importance and some had noticed cracks appearing in a highly romantic gesture that was, quite literally, out of this world. She told him she had bought him a star, which she named 'Jun'. This was a touching gesture. 'Romantic, isn't it?' reflected Depp later. 'I didn't know it was coming. I was completely surprised. I'd like to see it through a telescope. Get to know it. From what I know, it looks exactly like me. Same nostrils and all. It's amazing.' However, even this 'amazing' present could not paper over the cracks. A break was on the cards and Depp, so keen on the idea of romantic bliss, would, once again, be single.

There is a cruel irony in the fact that when Depp and Ryder had publicly discussed the possibility of their marriage they had always said it was just a matter of finding the right time, because it was, to a large extent, the *lack* of spare time that began the process that saw them split. Both the stars were facing the pressures that come with a golden run of film parts as their stars rose and rose.

•

For Ryder, these times were particularly demanding. Following her appearance in *Edward Scissorhands* she appeared in *Mermaids*, a comedy drama in which she appeared alongside Bob Hoskins and Cher. The film was shot in Boston, in the middle of a harshly cold winter. More importantly, Boston was a long way from Depp who was, meanwhile, filming in Vancouver. Though he flew to Boston to be with with Ryder as often as he could, it was a difficult period for them both. 'Man, I was a world-weary traveller,' said Depp of his regular journeying to be at his love's side.

Depp was busy, too, most significantly with two new films but he was also dipping his feet back into the rock music pool. 'Into The Great Wide Open' is a single lifted by Tom Petty and the Heartbreakers from their 1991 album of the same name. The promotional video for the song was directed by Julien Temple, who made his name directing films for punk band the Sex Pistols in the 1970s. For the lead protagonists in the video, Temple hired Johnny Depp and Faye Dunaway. Depp plays Eddie Rebel, a high school graduate who arrives in Hollywood full of dreams. Soon the excitement of the area goes to his head. Another promotional video Depp participated in around this time was for indie band The Lemonheads' single 'It's A Shame About Ray'.

Shooting for these videos took place during breaks from filming movies, the first of which was called *Arizona Dream*. Directed by Emir Kusturica, whose previous film, *Time of the Gypsies* Depp had adored, this film constituted just the sort of credibility-filled venture that Depp was seeking. Including pet turtles, a symbolic halibut and other oddball features, *Arizona Dream* was not one for a mainstream audience but ideal for viewers who wanted a film that was quite, but not too, intellectual and offbeat.

Depp played Axel Blackmar in this comic fantasy flick, an orphan who is taken under his uncle's wing and who then meets two interesting women, one of them played by Faye Dunaway. The *San Francisco Chronicle* called the film an 'inspired, erratic goulash that ignores standard movie-making formulas', while the *Los Angeles*

Times concluded, with similar rich vocabulary, that the film was 'a dazzling , daring slice of cockamamie'.

During the making of the film, Depp and Kusturica became thick as thieves. 'It was almost like a love affair,' said co-star Vincent Gallo, with a less than admiring tone. 'Emir and Johnny carried round Dostoevsky and Kerouac books and wore black. They had never worn black in their lives.' The pair also reportedly partied late into the night with their loud music and rowdy, drink-fuelled behaviour. Not that Gallo doubted Depp's behaviour in front of the camera. He was particularly in awe of how potently Depp played the silent scenes. 'Johnny is flawless,' he said, speaking of one such scene that is set in a cinema. 'He blows me off the screen, and it's my most animated scene in the film.'

Off screen, things were less stable for the film, which went through numerous name changes, walkouts and tantrums from the crew, as well as grave budget issues. It is something of a miracle the film ever got finished – and even then it did not get officially released in America.

Straight from the making of *Arizona Dream*, Depp worked on a new film called *Benny & Joon*, directed by Jeremiah Chechik. As with some of his earlier movies, he had not been the original choice to take the lead role, as Sam. Instead, that was to be taken by Tom Hanks, with Julia Roberts as his opposite number. Eventually, though, Depp took the male lead, alongside Mary Stuart Masterson. Depp's character was a fan of silent cinema, meaning Depp was again motivated to study the genre in preparation for filming.

'When I first met Johnny to discuss *Benny & Joon*,' said Chechik, 'I began to understand how much he brought to the role of *Edward Scissorhands*. He is so emotionally expressive, doing what seems to be so little. It was clear that he would bring a thoroughly original and exciting energy to the role of Sam.' Once more, Depp had won it at the audition. On set, he gave a winning performance – one for which he would be nominated for a Golden Globe.

He also drew admiring comments from the critics. As far as *Variety* was concerned, Depp was not just the making of the film, he was also its saviour. '[He] renders a startling performance that elevates the romantic fable way above its writing and directing shortcomings,' wrote Emmanuel Levy.

Roger Ebert of the *Chicago Times* struck a similar note in his write-up. He wrote that Depp 'takes a character that might have seemed unplayable on paper, and makes him into a kind of enchanter.' *The Mail on Sunday* described his performance as 'tenderly' delivered, and said his part was 'delightfully played'. Meanwhile, The *Spectator* magazine praised Depp as 'charming', adding that 'the charm is not forced'.

Taking on his next part seemed like a good idea at the time, but it is speculated that the pressure of the film, combined with his increasingly unsettled times with Ryder, sent him into a dark, despairing place. By his own admission, Johnny responded to this low point by drinking a lot, and also taking pills. Not that anyone who has seen the film in question would have any idea of his suffering, for Depp turned in another splendid performance.

When director Lasse Hallström had seen *Arizona Dream*, he was so blown away by Depp – who he thought put in a 'subtle and honest' performance in the film – that he made a note to try and hire him for the leading role in his next film, *What's Eating Gilbert Grape*. The director was surprised by Depp's appearance when they first met in person. 'He comes with a physical beauty that's just astonishing and at the same time he has no interest being that,' he said of Depp, who turned up with very long hair. Nevertheless, he impressed the director. For Hallström, it was 'the way [Depp] can convey sad emotions through his eyes', that he most liked.

This was to be an important skill to have in what would be arguably Depp's most challenging role to date. This eccentric, touching film charms the viewers thanks to Depp's portrayal of a man with a quiet sense of duty and loyalty, who has both qualities tested by a new woman who arrives in the little town in which he lives with his obese mother and his mentally ill younger brother, Arnie.

'Gilbert never really had the opportunity to go and make his life,' Depp told *GQ* magazine of his character in the film, which was based on a novel by Peter Hedges. 'He had to take care of his mom and his retarded brother.' For Depp, he wanted to journey deep into the soul of his character. Only down there, he felt, could he truly connect with what the character was going through, and by relating it to his own experiences, more sincerely tackle the part. Depp wanted to search for 'the hostility and rage' that Gilbert only displays on a couple of occasions during the story. 'I can understand the rage with wanting to completely escape from it and from everybody and everything you know and start a new life,' said Depp.

Hallström was pleased and a little surprised by how well his lead connected with the character he had created. 'Johnny Depp tapped the inner rage of that character and he knew even more about that character than I realized,' he said in 2006.

The admiration was mutual; Depp spoke with visceral admiration for the offbeat methods the film's director used. 'My character's uneasy with people so, like, if something gets too serious on the set, like if I'm feeling, "God, I'm doing a scene," Lasse automatically starts talking about radishes to get me back into how uncomfortable my character is,' he told *Movieline* magazine. 'Lasse says stuff like, "If a radish were up your butt, how far would it be? All the way in? Halfway? Just entering?" A radish is a pretty solid image, you know? So, that's how he communicates. He's allergic to bullsh*t.'

The 'radish method' deserves a place in movie folklore, surely. It certainly worked for Depp who was mesmerizing as Gilbert Grape. It is impossible to conceive that another actor could have nailed the part as convincingly as he did. His co-star Leonardo DiCaprio said, 'He was extremely like Gilbert, but it wasn't something Johnny was trying to do. It naturally came out of him. I never quite understood what he was going through because it wasn't some big emotional drama that was happening on the set.'

There were happy times off-set for the two actors. DiCaprio had been hired contrary to the initial plans of the film-makers. They had set out to find a young actor who was not especially good-looking. DiCaprio, though a confirmed pin-up, so impressed them with his audition that they gave him the part as Depp's brother. The two struck up something resembling a fraternal relationship off screen, too. The younger actor said they were 'buddy-buddy with each other'. Expanding on this, he explained that to have a true, brotherly understanding can be a quiet thing. 'They can just sit in a room and be together and just be completely comfortable with each other.'

Depp became fascinated by DiCaprio's facial expressions, not least the one he used when he was repulsed by something. In fact, Depp was so impressed with this that he kept hovering smelly things under DiCaprio's nose, in order to provoke the response. In the end, Depp had to pay for the privilege. Having regularly asked his younger co-star to smell everything from pickled sausage to rotten honeycomb and off-eggs, in order to study his gagging reflex, Depp soon found the experience more fun than DiCaprio. 'In the end, I couldn't stand it and I charged him for the pleasure,' said DiCaprio. 'I made about $500!'

However, the pain that Depp was going through mentally was impossible for him to escape. Hallström had been fearful that the character would 'cut a little close to home' for his star, and so it seemed to prove. '*Gilbert Grape* was a rough time for me just in terms of I didn't know where I was, emotionally or psychologically,' Depp said. Later, in an interview with *GQ* magazine, he talked about life during the filming. 'I poisoned myself constantly: drinking, didn't eat right, no sleep, lots of cigarettes. It was really a lonely, really f*cking lonely, time.' It wasn't just alcohol and tobacco that Depp was consuming. 'There were drugs, too,' he admitted in an interview with *Playboy* magazine. 'Pills. And there was a danger that I would go over the edge. I could have, I thank God I didn't.'

Perhaps this is the reason that he chose to not watch the film once it was made. He sometimes enjoys seeing himself on screen, but not with *Gilbert Grape*. Here, he was in a totally different mindset to when he was that excited youngster, sneaking into a test screening of his debut film *A Nightmare on Elm Street*. He said that he 'just didn't feel the need to see it' and so avoided doing so. Some time later, however, it came on the television unexpectedly. Depp tried to stick it out, but lasted no time at all. 'It was the opening credits and then the opening scene, and it got me to the point, I was trying to watch a little bit of it and I started to hyperventilate. I just shut the TV off and walked away.'

By not watching *Gilbert Grape* he missed out on a treat of a film, which continues to delight viewers to this day. In closing this section of his career, Hallström's verdict was interesting. '[Depp] has real ambitions, but he is deeply afraid of being considered pretentious,' he said. He has struggled less with this dichotomy since, but back in those days this issue gnawed away at him.

Meanwhile, Winona Ryder was still keeping just as busy. Next up for her came a spot in cult director Jim Jarmusch's vignette-ensemble film *Night on Earth*, from where she went straight on to Francis Ford Coppola's production of *Dracula* and on to another film, the Danish movie *The House of Spirits*. Amid all this, she also starred in *The Age of Innocence*, in which she played a socialite, but not before she had recognized the toll all this work had had on her.

It is far from unheard of for celebrities to seek the peace of rehab or even to enter into psychological treatment, and exhausted and upset, Ryder found herself at the door of a psychiatric unit. Serial insomnia had pushed her uncomfortably close to the brink. However, just five days later she checked out again. 'I just realized that no matter how much money you pay,' Ryder said later, during a cover feature interview with *Rolling Stone* magazine, 'these places don't have the answers. Because there are no answers. You're just a human being, and you make a choice to go on with your life.'

All the same, it was a very worrying mark of the stress she was under. With Depp also suffering from the intense pressure of work, the pair were of little support to one another just when mutual support was needed. They were instead, as one commentator described them, 'alone together'.

In the circumstances, the relationship was, to all intents and purposes, over long before the split became official. In those unhappy days, Ryder recalls a moment of poignant irony towards the end of the relationship. Suffering as ever from insomnia, she went on a night-time drive. As she drove, she saw a large poster that read: 'Winona Ryder: The Luckiest Girl in the World'. It was a painful moment for her as she realized that though she might be the envy of many women thanks to her relationship with Depp and movieland success, she felt anything but lucky. She had lost her way in life and was sure that ending her relationship with him was an important first step in getting back on the right path.

The increasing pressure from the media did not help at all, with many journalists regularly delighting in speculating that one or other of the lovers were 'playing away'. And if it could be suggested that the other party in the cheat was another famous movie star, then all the better. The fact that the stories had no foundation in truth was of less concern to the media. Ryder was rumoured to be having a fling with Daniel Day-Lewis, for instance. These stories were gold dust for the press, and the denial issued by Ryder came only after millions of people had already read the rumour.

'We couldn't go a week without reading something that either wasn't true or was only half true, or was taken out of context,' said Ryder, looking back in dismay. However, with a sense of relief, she added: 'I wouldn't want to go through that again. Looking back, I can see that it did affect our relationship. I was at an age when I was really insecure.' She had since dated other famous men, including actor Matt Damon. With the benefit of experience and maturity, she has become better able to deal with the attention and issues such relationships bring.

Early in their relationship, Depp and Ryder had decided to try and co-operate with the media in the hope the press would then back off. 'My relationship with Winona, it was my mistake to be as open as we were, but I thought if we were honest it would destroy that curiosity monster,' Depp told the *LA Times*. 'Instead it fed it, gave people license to feel they were part of it.' In retrospect, their ploy to fend off the media seems naive, and ever-destined to have failed.

Both Depp and Ryder share a character trait that makes them unlikely stars, not at ease with the attention and adulation that comes with mainstream Hollywood success. In today's climate of reality television shows, with members of the public queuing up to declare that becoming famous 'means more to me than anything', it is worth recalling that many stars only shine with a large dose of reluctance. Depp continued to struggle with the pressures of fame, and memorably recounted an example of one of those incidents during an interview with *Movieline* magazine. 'So, you're in a bar and you go to the bathroom to take a pee, right?' he said, 'and you're standing at the urinal with your dick in your hand and some guy comes up to you and goes, "Hey, so how are you and Winona doing?" I mean, Jesus Christ.'

As to that relationship, it is indeed believed to have been all but finished long before the split became official. 'He's a special guy,' said Ryder of her now ex-partner. 'I was just really young. I don't know what his excuse is, but that's mine.' She took the split hard and later said that she spent two weeks in a hotel room, drinking, smoking and listening to sad music, such as that of gloomy blues singer Tom Waits. According to some reports, she fell asleep with a lit cigarette in her hands and woke perilously close to the sort of disaster that has killed others, including rock singer Steve Marriott.

As for Depp, his first official public words on the split came in June 1993. 'It's never easy to cut the string, to sever the connection,' he said. 'But, with us, it just came to seem the natural thing to do . . . something that had to happen.' He confirmed that the split was relatively amicable. 'We're still friends, we still talk. And everything's fine, very amicable, very nice.'

A less positive spin was put on the break-up from a friend of Depp's, who claimed the actor was in denial about the split for some time after it happened. In the meantime, there was a rather awkward relic from the relationship that Depp to face up to and deal with: his split from Ryder was most symbolically marked by a change in one of his tattoos. Having had the words 'Winona Forever' tattooed on his arm during the early stages of their relationship, clearly, that had to go.

However, instead of removing it altogether he opted for a clever edit. From now on, it would read simply: 'Wino Forever'. Depp's drinking had been a source of concern for some time among some of those close to him. He was speaking of going through 'an ugly, ugly time'.

Since he first read *On the Road*, the novel inspired by the Beat generation, no stranger to narcotics and excessive alcohol use themselves, Johnny has proved himself more than capable of partying hard. Much of the music that he has enjoyed over the years is also of the type that is fuelled by and celebrates narcissism. For instance, he rates 'Rum, Sodomy & The Lash' by The Pogues as one of his favourite albums of all time. 'Feral, beautiful poetry from one of our century's greatest poets,' he gushed of their second, immensely enjoyable album. 'A grand testament to love, adventure, and hedonism! Shane MacGowan is Brendan Behan's dream come true!'

Since he first emerged as a musician with The Nipple Erectors in the 1970s, and then formed The Pogues in the 1980s, MacGowan has been almost certainly the most hedonistic artist of his generation. This is, after all, the man who was told, even by notorious caner Keith Richards of the Rolling Stones to 'take it easy a bit'. To this day, MacGowan's songs are celebrations of life on the partying edge. Depp is also a fan of the similarly-sodden Tom Waits. 'The Devil doesn't have the best tunes – Tom Waits does,' he said. The growling Waits voice was described as sounding 'like it was soaked in a vat of bourbon, left hanging in the smokehouse for a few months, and then taken outside and run over with a car', by one critic.

With the tunes of these artists filling his head, it must have felt all the more natural for Depp to hide from the pain he was feeling, from the 'ugly, ugly time' he was going through, with yet more bottles of liquor. By his own admission, he was poisoning himself. He has never said that he had a genuine death wish at this time, but he was teetering in a dark place. During one interview, he made an abrupt observation that seemed dark, as well as random. 'My goldfish are dead,' he said during the interview with *GQ*. 'It just hit me. That I had some goldfish, they were on that table. About four or five days ago one died, then a couple days later – no, yesterday – the other died. Yeah, goldfish die quick. Or maybe they die slow, but to you it seems quick.' At the same time, he spoke to the Australian edition of *Cosmopolitan* magazine, speaking wistfully of deep sleep. 'Really deep, you're just loving it, lying there, a trance,' he said. Even director Emir Kusturica observed of Depp that 'he has a certain self-destructive side'.

Perhaps it is the astonishing level of empathy that Depp has to summon in order to capture his characters so successfully that is partially responsible for his ability to go through such despair. As he once told an interviewer, he feels he can, in everyday life, notice instances of unhappiness in others. 'It sounds stupid, but you see that woman sitting over there, eating?' he asked Chris Heath, interviewing him for *Details* magazine. 'There's something sad about that. You look a little closer, and you see the way she's cutting her meat. And the way she puts the fork into the food and takes a bite. And the way she's chewing. You know? Normal, everyday things. But I see that . . . and I could cry my eyes out.'

As he sunk ever lower, however, he suddenly reached a plateau where he realized that things were actually so much better than he thought. There was no need, he decided, to keep drinking and feeling so low. He thought of how much he had going for him. Certainly, for most ordinary folk it was easy to see how much he had on his side. Good looks, growing riches and a movie career that reflected his immense talent – plenty of mere mortals would never frown again if they could land those three things. He may have lost sight of his good fortune for a while but, as before, he came back to his senses before it was too late. 'So I stopped everything for the better part of a year,' he said. 'I guess I just reached a point where I said, "Jesus Christ, what am I doing? Life is fucking good! What am I doing to myself?"'

Vincent Gallo made a straight-talking summary of

the issues he, and some others, felt Depp was facing in *Neon* Magazine. 'The exterior, the TV pop star turned bad boy, waif lover, hipster friend of Jim Jarmusch, is totally uninteresting,' he said. 'It's tragic that he has this poser part of himself, that he has to invent himself like that. If only he would allow himself to be who he really is, somebody who's traumatized and trapped by his childhood and emotional life, then he would be interesting, a great person, a great talent. He is one of the most funny, talented, likeable, sweet authentic people I've ever met.' These words may seem damning, but were underpinned by an essential warmth and respect for Depp, a man wrestling with a number of identities. Such a fate is the danger many actors face. How could it not be, as they move from part to part, role to role, often with little respite between to reconnect with who they really are?

It is worth noting the films that Depp turned down, as well as the ones in which he participated. Among the better known of those he rejected were *Interview with the Vampire* (the part he was offered later went to Tom Cruise) and Bruce Willis's part in *Hudson Hawk*, as well as the lead role – eventually taken by Leonardo DiCaprio – in *Titanic*. He also turned down a part in the blockbuster *Speed*. Without being specific, he has admitted that he later regretted turning down some parts during his career.

For Depp, these decisions confirmed that he had artistic and creative credibility; for his agent, it might have been a different feeling. It would be a saintly agent who would not mourn losing their 'ten per cent' on such deals. However, Jacobs insisted she was not troubled by his decisions and that a more commercially rewarding film would come along for him one day. 'Am I disappointed that he turned those projects down? No. Do I want him to be in a movie that does $400 million? Of course – I'm not stupid! Let me make this really clear to you: he wants to be in a commercial movie. It just has to be the right timing, and the right one, that's all! Hopefully he'll be available when those come along again.'

In the meantime, the parts he was taking were less mainstream and 'obvious' than the likes of *Speed* or *Interview with the Vampire*. 'I'm not a blockbuster boy,' he explained. 'I just don't want to look back in thirty or forty or fifty years and have my grandkids say, "What an idiot you were, smiling for the cameras and playing the game".' There was a danger at this stage of his acting career that, in trying to avoid being typecast in a mainstream part, he instead became typecast as one who will or can only player outsider, eccentric roles in offbeat movies. 'Will he still be playing kooks when he's forty?' asked *Sky* magazine. It is hard for any actor to win, sometimes. Had he taken the easy route and chosen a succession of mainstream parts in commercial movies, he would have been criticized for vulgar laziness. By taking a more imaginative, challenging and interesting route, he was not immune to criticism anyway.

Not that Depp cared one bit. He kept the whole issue in perspective, and refused to conform to 'luvvie' stereotypes. 'People have mentioned that I like doing offbeat roles, but I've been lucky in the sense that I haven't been typecast,' he insisted. 'It's important to keep changing. There's a lot of stuff that I just don't buy into, like being an actor who takes himself so seriously that he pretends to be a tortured artist.' He added that actors do not necessarily experience more pain than anyone else in life.

This was a refreshing sentiment to come out of Hollywood, and one that played well with the public. Those who work hard in 'everyday' jobs to earn modest wages that take care of little more than life's basic necessities have grown increasingly bored of hearing showbusiness folk complain about how hard their lives are. Just how hard can it be, people wonder, to earn big bucks for doing what seems like minimal work, before retiring by a pool in the California sunshine? True, he had experienced some hardships and sorrows, but he was realistic enough to count his blessings at this stage in his life. This was just as well, for he had some testing times ahead of him.

CHAPTER FOUR:

SUCCESS AND TRAGEDY

'I think I would have been as sick as a dog if I had walked away from this one,' said Depp of the next major film proposal he received. It was time for him to team up with Tim Burton again. 'I feel close to Johnny,' Burton said once, 'because I think somewhere inside we respond to similar things.'

In a director/actor relationship that was threatening to become as close and full of rapport as that between Martin Scorcese and Robert De Niro, the pair were to be the centre of another great offbeat cinematic triumph, *Ed Wood*. The film was about the influential cult film director Edward D. Wood Jnr. His heyday had come in the 1950s, when he was behind a string of fascinating films including *Glen or Glenda* and *Plan 9 From Outer Space*. Many of the movies Wood Jnr made starred the actor Bela Lugosi. Wood Jnr was also known for his transvestism. When Burton first called Depp to sound him out about the part, the decision process was fast: they met twenty minutes later in a Los Angeles bar and by the time they had left, Depp had agreed to play Wood in the film.

He expected it to be a challenge – and it was. Johnny began his preparation by researching everything he could about transvestism, and his research took him to strange places. 'I'm telling you, being a woman is hard,' he said with a chuckle. 'You've got all the make-up and bras and stuff – it's a lot of work. You can never fully understand what it's like to be a woman until you have to wear those clothes. And playing a transvestite is even harder. You have to make a real commitment to it. You have to hide stuff and tuck it away and it's really quite painful. I'm telling you, I have a lot of respect for transvestites.'

Soon he found it easier to be in costume, so much so that he was reported to have gone out for a drink in costume at one point. Asked by *Seventeen* magazine if playing a woman would make him a more considerate boyfriend in future, Depp was happy to go along with the theme. 'Absolutely,' he said. '*Ed Wood* made me realize exactly what girls go through to get dolled up for a date. Guys just shower, put on some clothes, maybe shave. All guys should try to put on pantyhose just once.'

Once again, Depp took the role very seriously and dressed in women's clothing ahead of filming so as to become comfortable with the part, rather than to express any part of himself. He quipped that during his teens he dated a girl who wore an Angora jumper and that when they split up he missed the jumper more than the girl. One day he received a parcel from a finishing school in New York that instructs men on how to behave like women. 'It was a bunch of stuff, literature and photographs,' he remembered, together with a letter promising him that they could 'help you become a woman'. Depp considered taking them up on the offer, but is believed to have turned it down. He is not a method actor, in the generally understood sense of that term, as he explained with passion to *Playboy* magazine. 'I don't buy it when a guy says, "You must call me Henry the Eighth. Even when I go get a Dr Pepper I am Henry the Eighth!",' he said. 'I can't see that. If you're truly in character it becomes unconscious. If you realize you're in character or say you are, then you're fucked. It means that you're satisfied, and that's the worst.'

However, when Edward Wood Jnr's widow Cathy visited the set she felt Depp had the part licked. 'I would be standing there in a dress and she would look at me like I was totally normal,' said Depp. 'One day she said, "Johnny, you look nice. You look like Eddie." That made me very happy.'

He wondered whether or not he made for an attractive woman. 'When I first looked in the mirror, I thought I was the ugliest woman I had ever seen. I mean, I looked huge in those clothes!' He became increasingly shy and picky about who was around when he changed costume, hinting at understandable discomfort. Others, though, felt he made a good job of playing a woman. 'Johnny was so credible that he pulls it off without making it laughable,' said Burton. 'Besides, he really looks great in those clothes.'

Depp's costume designer said that transforming his look for the drag scenes was an easy task. 'When he's a woman, we pad out his hips and give him a bust and stuff,' said Colleen Atwood. 'Actually Johnny looks great as a woman . . . We were saying: "God, he's beautiful."' In time, Depp became more and more comfortable in the costumes he had to wear. 'It was spookily comfortable,' he admitted. 'I am getting better at walking in high heels.'

This was not just the first time Johnny played a character in drag; it was also the first time that Depp had portrayed a real person on screen, rather than a fictional character. He decided to base his interpretation on a combination of Casey Kasem, Ronald Reagan and the Tin Man character from *The Wizard of Oz*. He was realistic enough to know that there was no way he would be able to completely faithfully represent a man who was no longer alive, and of whom there was precious little footage. That said, he was comfortable that they had made a sincere and decent job of the challenge.

'This is an homage,' he said of *Ed Wood*. 'A real weird homage, but nevertheless a respectable one.' He felt kinship in some areas with Wood, a man who he felt was 'not afraid to take chances', and one that 'did exactly what he wanted to'. Furthermore, he attributed Wood with 'images that were surreal, with moments of genius'. Most of all, he hoped that his part in the film would help Wood be remembered the right way, not for anything controversial or seedy, but 'as an artist'.

When it was released in the autumn of 1994, *Ed Wood* was not a commercial success to say the least. Following its premiere at the New York Film Festival at the Lincoln Center it went on general release in America at the end of September. It is thought to have taken less than $6 million, which was far below its $18 million budget. Perhaps this was the only fitting financial result for a film about a man who broke rules, shattered boundaries and was a hero, but only as a 'cult' director.

Might Wood have turned in his grave had his film become too successful in mainstream circles? It was a hit with the critics, for sure. Calling *Ed Wood* 'Burton's most personal and provocative movie to date,' *Rolling Stone* magazine's Peter Travers kicked off a slew of admiring reviews from the hard-to-please ladies and gentlemen of the press. Janet Maslin of The *New York Times* said the film confirmed that Depp is a 'certified great actor'. *Entertainment Weekly* struck a similar chord, saying that in *Ed Wood* Depp established himself as 'an exemplary actor' and *Premiere* magazine described Depp's part as 'another *Edward Scissorhands*'. The most noteworthy negative review came from *Time* magazine, which wondered why Burton had created such a 'dishwatery' film.

British viewers had to wait until late spring 1995 until they could see the film. Again, it fared modestly in commercial terms but excited the critics, one of which described Depp's performance as 'truly mesmerizing'.

Premiere magazine made a valid comparison between *Ed Wood* and *Edward Scissorhands*, but one media interviewer got the two mixed up in a less intelligent manner. When Depp told a German interviewer that his next role was going to be as Ed Wood, the interviewer replied he had never heard of Wood. Depp, surprised by this, repeated the name 'Ed Wood' more carefully. 'Oh, Edward Scissorhands!' said the interviewer, believing he now understood. 'No,' replied Depp with admirable calm, 'I've already done that one.' Depp has always done his best to remain calm and kind during such interviews, but in truth his patience is often tested to near its limit.

The film did well at award ceremonies. Martin Landau won Best Actor at the 1995 Academy Awards for his part in the film, and it also won Best Make-Up at the same ceremony. Landau also won Best Supporting Actor at the first Screen Actors Guild Awards. Depp was nominated for a Golden Globe for Best Actor in a Musical or Comedy for his portrayal of Ed Wood, but he did not win the award.

However, he found the filming for the movie a 'great exorcism' after so many dark days. 'It was the end of something, and the beginning of something else.' As he exorcized the darkness, he also knocked drinking on the head for some months. He felt happy again – happy and healthy.

•

Not that he was about to go all mainstream and normal on us. The more peculiar parts of Depp's nature remained consistent during ups and downs, and the days of wild indulgence and sober serenity. In the early to mid-1990s Depp collected a series of weird and wonderful items to keep in his house. Among his hoard of eccentricity were lacquered piranhas, a stuffed bat, a genie lamp and some clown posters. 'Clowns have always scared me, so I think if I surround myself with them, it'll ward off evil.'

Another long-standing phobia was tested when a friend bought Depp a tarantula spider as a gift. The arachnophobic Depp said: 'I thought, well, this is great. Now maybe I won't be scared of them anymore. So I'd try to touch him and when I did, I'd scream, so I had to get rid of him.'

On his wall were also mounted dead insects. 'Bugs', said Depp, 'are so mysterious. We don't know how or what they are. They just are.' He also bought a nine-foot rooster made out of fibre glass. 'I always thought it was good to say that I had the biggest cock in Los Angeles,' he said. Together, these belongings made for a strange collection, to say the least. 'Various places,' he replied when asked where he got them from. 'For instance, there's an amazing bug store I go to in Paris, which is also where I got my pigeon skeleton.' He admitted that bringing such strange purchases back to America could prove complicated. 'It can be a bitch with customs,' he said. He remembered a time he was stopped in customs by a burly officer. 'So, what do we have in the bag?' the officer asked Depp. The actor replied: 'Well, I've got some books, clothes, dead piranhas and a bat.' Continuing the story, he said: 'At that point, they searched every nook and cranny. It was hell, but hey – at least I didn't have to pay duty.'

The outgoing message on his answerphone was also a bit 'out there' at this point. It consisted of a recording of a hypnotist telling a patient: 'Your breasts are starting to tingle now . . . You can feel your breasts starting to tingle . . . A sensation of growth is taking place!' Strange stuff, but no more strange than some of the choices of pseudonyms he used to check quietly into hotels. The most memorable one reported was, 'Mr Donkey Penis', though Depp has contested that he ever used that one. He has readily confessed, though, to checking in under a host of other names including 'Santa Del Vecchio, The Reverend Something or other, even Oprah Noodlemantra . . .' Good fun, one supposes, though if his intention had been to avoid excessive attention from random women, he had chosen poorly. Soon, he would be the subject of a media storm as a result of something that happened in a hotel. First, though, he found himself the centre of an even graver controversy, as he was linked to one of the decade's most tragic Hollywood stories.

•

In the early months of 1993, Depp received a proposal that was to change his life, adding a new string to his ever-varied bow. It would give him a business interest in a Los Angeles nightclub that was ailing when he took over but soon became the place to be seen in the famous city.

The Central Nightclub stood in a prime Los Angeles location: on the corner of the fabled Sunset Boulevard and Larrabee Street. Appropriately for its location near Hollywood, the Central had been used as a shooting location on several occasions, including for the Oliver Stone film *The Doors*.

Despite this glamour, as 1993 began the club was struggling financially. After a conversation with two people involved with running the Central, Depp paid a reported $350,000 for a majority stake in the venue and found himself a club owner. Asked by *Sky* magazine why he went through with the deal, he said: 'Well, I like to hang out with musicians, and most Hollywood clubs are so boring I just figured that it would be more fun to start my own. I just wanted it to be low-key, but then it got real crazy for a while.'

With Depp as its owner, the fortunes of the place were to see a dramatic turnaround. Soon, it became a popular and hip place, soaring in attendance and takings. 'I never had any idea that it was going to do that,' said Depp. 'I really thought it was gonna just be this cool little underground place.' His relaunch gave the place a new name – The Viper Room – and it officially threw open its doors in August 1993. It was a proud evening for Depp as his ex-Pogues pal Shane MacGowan, backed by a local Irish band, toasted the new place on stage with a typically raucous set. Depp wallowed in the excitement of the evening as all his work in preparing for it came good. He had themed the venue on a Speakeasy bar, a throwback to the romantic days of Prohibition in the America of the 1920s. 'I'm fascinated with the beginning of Hollywood and what it must have been like in the twenties and thirties,' said Depp. 'I'm a real history freak.'

He was proud to throw his creativity into something as tangible and physical as a venue, rather than into music or film which, while sources of great pride for him, were perhaps less immediately rewarding as his own nightclub. As he opened its doors and watched excited, hip folk pouring through them, he felt a glow of pride. With good cause – it was said of The Viper Room that the audience were usually more famous than the performers. Soon, though, the venue would become infamous.

In the meantime, visitors were quick to praise the friendly vibe of the place, with one saying: 'There wasn't this insane man standing out front who was evil to people. Even though they did have a red rope, I don't think people felt as rejected. Everyone got in if there was room.' Depp arranged regular themed nights, including a dating evening in which a bachelor would be asked probing questions from potential partners. These were riotous, laughter-filled affairs. One such question was, 'I like to masturbate in my spare time for hours on end until I'm suicidal. What do you like to do for a hobby?'

On other evenings a succession of acts would perform. Naturally, given Depp's influence, these were frequently rather eccentric acts including a German bullwhip artist, a Christian Science ventriloquist, a Spanish Popeye and 'a mime that talks' called Enoch Cook. Who else but Depp could put together such a quirky line-up?

There had always been an unconventional air to the place, even prior to Depp buying it; it had been the venue for a regular Alcoholics Anonymous meeting. 'It was like therapy at the point of the problem,' quipped one observer. It became so achingly hip that Nancy

Sinatra, daughter of the legendary Frank, said, 'If my dad were still performing, he'd want to play an after-hours show there.'

Sometimes, long after the venue had closed its doors, Depp would perform solitary sets on the stage of the deserted venue, purely for his own entertainment. 'You've got a guy who, for all intents and purposes, is not taken seriously for what he's really in love with, so he ends up making a home for himself to have that, you know?' said Morty Coyle, a member of a local band and a regular Viper Room face. As well as the eccentric performers and Depp's after-hours slots, the venue also played host to famous performers including Johnny Cash, Mick Jagger and Lenny Kravitz.

There were sometimes malfunctions in the men's toilet, where only one urinal stood. 'It used to get wet,' Depp told *Details* magazine. He then spoke, with affection and wit, of a prankster who used to set up a messy trick in the toilets. 'There was a guy who would somehow sneak in here with a monkey wrench. He would loosen a nut on the urinal so that when the next person flushed, water would go everywhere. It was like Niagara Falls. You had people running from the bathroom, slipping, security guys sprinting over to throw down towels. This happened fairly regularly for weeks, and I came to respect the toilet guy. I liked his method, his consistency. He clearly took pride in toilet sabotage. But then it stopped, and I kind of miss him.'

This was not the only lavatorial mishap to hit the place. One night, as Morty Coyle recalled, a toilet roll holder got stuck in a toilet, prompting a star-studded investigation team. 'Johnny was with Kate Moss [by then his partner], and Sal [Jenco, co-owner of the club] was under the table – everybody's trying to get this thing out,' said Coyle. 'It was the weirdest thing in the world; they're all standing around a toilet bowl. And Kate gives her opinion on it, so to speak, and we all go, "Why don't you stick your arm in and grab the thing out?" And she goes to Johnny, "Would you give me $100 if I stick my hand in and take it out?" And he goes, "Yeah, because I can get $400 from the *National Enquirer* for a picture of you with your hand in a toilet."' In time the *National Enquirer* would be just one of hundreds of media outlets who were fighting to get exclusive stories from The Viper Room, after one of Hollywood's most iconic young stars met his death on its doorstep.

It was on 30 October 1993 that actor River Phoenix arrived at The Viper Room with his brother Leaf, sister Rain, girlfriend Samantha Mathis and friend 'Flea', the bassist in rock band Red Hot Chilli Peppers. It was a short visit. 'River was in the club for all of twenty-seven minutes,' said Depp. But they were twenty-seven fateful minutes. Soon after midnight that Phoenix complained that he felt ill.

'He kept leaping up and bumping into things,' said one member of the venue's staff. 'His words were so slurred you could barely understand him.' His friends helped him leave the club, hoping a breath of fresh air might help him. A call was made to the emergency services, in which Phoenix's brother pleaded: 'It's my brother. He's having seizures at Sunset and Larrabee. Please come here.' But before the ambulance arrived, Phoenix had died on the doorstep of Depp's club. He was pronounced dead at 1.51 a.m., the official cause being 'acute multiple drug ingestion'.

The ambulance team had tried to save his life, but could not. 'When we attached our cardiac monitor to him he was in a flatline, which meant that there was no heart activity whatsoever,' recalled Capt. Ray Ribar, LA County paramedic supervisor.

The world was stunned when news broke of this youth culture icon's passing. River Phoenix was just twenty-three years old and was considered one of the most promising actors of his generation. Indeed, although his contemporaries in age were the likes of Keanu Reeves and Christian Slater, given that he managed to combine undoubted good looks with cinematic integrity, he had more in common with Depp.

The two were fans of each other's work, and had ambitions to work together one day. Phoenix had had an unconventional childhood, raised by parents who were members of a religious cult called Children of God. He was named after the river of life in the Herman Hesse novel *Siddhartha*. He became an actor at the age of ten, appearing in films including *Stand By Me*, *Mosquito Coast* and as the young Indiana Jones in the *Last Crusade* instalment of the series. He said of his work as the 'younger Harrison Ford', 'I would just look at Harrison: he would do stuff and I would not mimic it, but interpret it younger.'

However, it was his role in *My Own Private Idaho* that saw River Phoenix assume the status of an icon to a generation of indie filmgoers. In the film, in which he played a narcoleptic rent boy, he and his co-star Keanu Reeves put in powerful performances. Both young men were stunningly good-looking, but their performances also oozed credibility. He also appeared in other films including *A Fish Called Wanda*, *A Thing Called Love* and *Sneakers*. In his final days he was working on a film called *Dark Blood in Utah*, and was also earmarked for a role in *Interview With the Vampire*. Everything was in place for Phoenix to have an extraordinary life. It was tragic that it came to such an abrupt and unpleasant end on the doorstep of The Viper Room.

Depp described how Phoenix had arrived at the venue that evening, with his guitar in one hand and his girlfriend on his other arm. 'He came to play and he didn't think he was going to die – nobody thinks they're

going to die. He wanted to have a good time.' Depp
argued that the fact Phoenix arrived with his guitar was
proof that he was not 'an unhappy kid', and that his
death was not some sort of cry for help gone wrong,
or even suicide. Furious at some of the rumours and
speculation that quickly began after the news broke,
Depp accused those who circulated such lies of 'trying
to tarnish the memory' of a 'very sweet guy who made
one fatal mistake'.

The following day, the venue became a shrine to
Phoenix. Fans arrived, left flowers and candles and
wrote messages of support and love to Phoenix on the
walls. Tributes were also made from the entertainment
world. 'He played my son once, and I came to love him
like a son, and was proud to watch him grow into a
man of such talent and integrity and compassion,' said
Harrison Ford in a statement. 'We will all miss him.'
Director Phil Alden Robinson, who directed Phoenix
in *Sneakers*, said: 'He was enormously talented. He
cared deeply about his craft. He loved to take chances.
He loved to dig deeper and push harder. He was an
extraordinarily honest actor. It's a great tragedy.'

Depp was understandably devastated and shaken.
Not only had he lost a dear friend, he also had to contend
with absurd and obscene headlines. For instance, the
News of the World described The Viper Room as 'Depp's
Den of Sex, Drugs And Death'. He was furious and

informed anyone who would listen that his venue was 'a decent place'. He railed against the tawdry tabloid speculation, which, he argued, was mostly ill-informed and groundless, the preserve of 'backyard detectives' and tabloid papers. 'It's really tragic and sad,' he said.

An aspect of the media coverage that particularly revolted him was the broadcasting and quoting of the call Phoenix's brother made to the emergency services on the evening. 'How many times did we need to hear that 911 tape?' wondered Depp. He mourned what this said about American society. 'We've become a society of ambulance chasers,' he said. 'Everybody focused on the bad; nobody's interested in the good.'

Turning specifically on some of the more sinister speculation, Depp was forthright. 'To say I opened a nightclub to allow people to do drugs, even in the bathroom – do people think I'm insane? Do they think I'm going to throw everything away – even my own children's future, so people could get high in a nightclub? It's ridiculous.' Anecdotal evidence supports Depp's protestations.

Morty Coyle revealed that he once saw Viper Room staff jump on two customers who were smoking a joint in the club. 'There are no drugs in The Viper Room,' he said. 'They had the disaster, but honestly, there are no drugs in there. It's for drinking and hanging out.' Meanwhile Depp wondered why people were so keen to focus on his club as the centre of all evil, rather than reflecting further on the tragedy of Phoenix's passing. 'To pinpoint one club or one street is really ridiculous,' he told *USA Today*. 'There's a tragic loss of a very gifted, very sweet, nice young man.'

Not for the last time in his life, Johnny found himself with an ongoing gripe against the media. 'This is my quarrel with the press – they could have said, "Look, this was a normal guy, who had some things he was confused about, and he made a mistake, and it could have been any of us. Watch yourself." But nobody said that.'

He closed The Viper Room for a fortnight and during that time young fans of Phoenix continued to turn the outside of the club into a shrine for their hero. On reopening he continued to close the venue on every anniversary of Phoenix's passing until he sold his interest in the club.

It is a mark of Phoenix's stature and talent that he has remained as famous in death as he had in life, if not more so. As for Depp's venue, the discussion of what part it played in the story continued, occasionally taking on some genuinely bizarre tones. For instance, people have since suggested that The Viper Room might be cursed. As evidence for this sinister theory they point out that in addition to Phoenix's death, a previous owner of the venue died while in the job; also that both Michael Hutchence and Timothy Leary died just days after performing at the venue.

Reflecting on the sorry saga in a later press interview, Depp took a wider look at the issue of drugs and their place in American society. 'If you're talking about drugs, you're talking about America,' he told *Sky* magazine. 'People die from drug overdoses every single day. You can't say specifically Hollywood or Sunset Boulevard. The problem is everywhere, and it's been going on for thirty years at least. And the people benefiting from the drugs are very rich, and it's a huge business. So let's not pretend. The problem is not necessarily on the streets with the kids. Though there's a lot of curious kids who will try this and try that. The real problem is way up there – with the higher-ups. The upper, upper echelon.'

Given the direction that Phoenix's career was taking, it is not inaccurate to say that he could have become Hollywood's other Johnny Depp. He had pin-up looks, which he could use to his advantage, but which he was never keen to overplay or rely on. As such, he made for an engrossing character, a handsome hero for indie-film fans who didn't mind dipping a toe into the more mainstream end of the cinematic pool from time to time. Yet drugs had robbed the world of Phoenix. Had Depp ever sailed close to such an untimely end? Once more, in the wake of the tragedy, he admitted that he had taken drugs and had made many mistakes along the way. Why, then, had he not succumbed to tragedy as

Phoenix had done? 'I saw it was enough,' he said. 'And luckily, I had friends and family who saw a different side of me that wanted to be saved."

Depp has been involved in anti-drugs initiatives, and in February 1994 he attended a party in Los Angeles that was raising funds for a drugs education programme. During the evening, he showed a short film he had directed to educate people on the dangers of drugs. The woman on his arm that night was a beautiful, famous model.

Her name? Kate Moss.

CHAPTER FIVE:

GOOD DAYS, BAD DAYS

A confirmed romantic, whenever Depp has spoken of the first time he met some of the women he has dated, it has been a tale full of drama and sudden lust. When he met Kate Moss, it was a more everyday encounter.

Born in Croydon in 1974, Moss went on to become one of the world's biggest supermodels and a true fashion icon. It was while she was passing time between flights at JFK airport in New York at the age of fourteen that she was first spotted, by the founder of the Storm model agency, Sarah Doukas. Moss recognized Doukas and was delighted to be asked to model for the agency.

Within a year she was gracing catwalks around the world and by the time she was eighteen she appeared on the cover of influential magazine *The Face* and was soon globally renowned and the face of Calvin Klein. Men's magazines regularly voted her at the top of their 'sexiest woman of the year' polls, reflecting the feverish admiration their readers had for this stunning beauty. In modelling circles she became synonymous with the waif look, in reference to her eternally slender figure, which stood in stark contrast to the more buxom and curvaceous look that had been popular for so long.

So she made for quite a sight when Depp first met her in New York City in January 1994. They first met at Café Tabac in Manhattan. Moss had popped over to the city that never sleeps through work, and it just so happened that Depp was visiting the Big Apple at the same time. This time, Johnny was more matter-of-fact about their first meeting. 'It wasn't all that romantic,' he recalled. 'She was sitting at a table with some friends, and I knew one of them.' Hardly the 'love at first sight' stuff of old for Depp – and Moss explained that it was not a 'love at first sight' experience for her, either. 'No, not the first moment I saw him,' she said. However, she added that there was a lesser certainty from the start. 'I knew from the first moment we talked that we were going to be together. I've never had that before.' She later admitted that 'I fancied him before I met him!'

As for Depp, once they were an item he would regularly see huge billboards with his girlfriend plastered beautifully across them. 'I think she's beautiful,' he said. 'Calvin Klein is lucky to have her. If we're apart and I see her picture I'll miss her, not because of a billboard but because she's always on my mind anyway.'

Having dated other famous women in his life, including Winona Ryder, once he began dating Moss, Depp was asked why famous people so often only dated other stars. For him, the answer was straightforward. 'Probably because you have mutual friends,' he said. 'You move in the same circles. It's like working in a factory – you strike up friendships with other employees. Also, you'll go to a restaurant or a bar that caters to other people who know what it's like to be exposed. So maybe they're not after you so much.'

Lots of women around the globe fancied Depp at this time, but not all of them got to meet him as Moss had. As they became involved, though, Depp quickly became besotted with her. He tried to speak with serenity about their relationship, but there was no hiding his admiration. 'We're just having fun, a lot of fun,' he said. 'She's a real down-to-earth English girl who gives me no chance to get big-headed about my life.' He also told *FHM* that her feet were the part of her body, rather than more obvious ones, that he was most taken with. 'They are very, very important,' he said. He added that a favourite date for them was at the Magic Mountain theme park, near Los Angeles, where they would go on 'all the fastest rides'. They were also seen partying with Oasis guitarist and songwriter Noel Gallagher, whose then wife, Meg Matthews, was just the sort of woman Moss loved to socialize with.

Naturally, not everyone was enamoured of Depp's new partner. Models, particularly the female of the species, have always been viewed with cynicism by others. It is as if the world is only willing to cope with extreme beauty by detracting from the other qualities of those who possess it. Also, given the large age gap between them – nearly eleven years – it was easy to sneer. So some people who knew Depp spoke of their relationship with some degree of doubt. 'I'm going to assume that [she must be great] and endow her with good qualities because I can't imagine Johnny spending time with anyone who wasn't his equal,' said Sarah Jessica Parker, who appeared in *Ed Wood* with him. For those who doubted their relationship, news that broke that autumn out of New York City must have seemed like confirmation of their worst fears.

●

A friend of his once described Johnny Depp as 'the most gentle, sweetest soul who ever walked the earth'. However, it was hard to square this image with the man who, on 13 September 1994, was led away by Manhattan police after violently trashing the hotel room in which he and Moss were staying. The incident took place at the $1,200 a night Mark Hotel in New York. However, the stay was ultimately going to cost him a whole lot more than that.

Less than a year after River Phoenix died on the doorstep of The Viper Room, Depp was once more back in the headlines for all the wrong reasons. This time there was no human harm or tragedy involved, but that did not stop Depp from being judged harshly.

The story begins a week earlier, with an incident in London. Depp was in town to meet Moss, when he reportedly became involved in a scuffle with another man, a twenty-seven-year-old photographer named Jonathan Walpole. It began, said Walpole, when he accidentally picked up Depp's drink at the bar. 'He pulled both my ears very hard,' Walpole told London's *Evening Standard*, adding that 'some ape' who was with Depp 'leaped on my back, put his arm round my neck and tried to force my head to the floor.' This painted the story one way, but a later article in *Icon* magazine was to suggest a whole different slant on what occurred. The article suggested that Depp had reacted more with valour than with malice, and only after Walpole had repeatedly badgered a friend of Moss.

Depp and Moss reportedly had previous form for arguments in hotels. Once, reports suggested that they had a huge row in a hotel lobby in America. 'It was in the papers,' said Depp. 'I thought it was pretty magical of us, for we were in France at the time.' However, not all the reports were similarly contested. Just three months before the Mark Hotel incident, the couple had shouted angrily at each other in the dining room of Manhattan's Royalton Hotel. This was to prove an awkward moment for them both once they had calmed down but the real drama was yet to come.

The Mark Hotel is an Upper East side venue of some stature, based on Madison Avenue near Manhattan's Museum District and with Central Park a mere saunter away. A classical 1920s building, the outside of the venue is impressive, but inside the decor quickly becomes modern and stylish from the lobby onwards. This was indeed a venue fit for a star, and was, therefore, the one that Depp was staying in while he completed his promotional duties surrounding the release of *Ed Wood*.

To keep him company, Moss checked in herself on 12 September and joined Depp in room 1410. Neither could have known how badly wrong the evening would go. At five the next morning guests were complaining of noise coming from room 1410. However this was not the noise of passion but of a bitter argument. Among those who complained was Roger Daltrey, the lead singer of British rock band The Who. Daltrey was in the room next to Depp and Moss; his call to reception informed them that there was a noisy argument combined with lots of noise of destruction taking place next door. A member of the hotel's security team, was sent straight to room 1410 to investigate. It was later claimed by Depp and others that the security guard 'had it in' for Depp before the trouble even started.

Certainly the man did not respond in the way Depp hoped he would. As far as the actor was concerned, once he had apologized for the noise and damage, and promised to pay for the latter, the matter should have been dropped. However, this was an unlikely hope, not least when one reads what the police listed as damaged in their report of the incident. Depp had, claimed the report, broken a pair of seventeenth-century photo frames, a Chinese pot, a lamp stand and a glass tabletop. The police also reported finding some broken coffee table legs, a broken flower vase and several cigarette burns in the suite's expensive carpet.

'It's someone else's property and you have got to respect that,' said Depp with some element of contrition. However, he was later to play the whole business down, saying: 'I had to go to jail for assaulting a picture frame and a lamp!' Even if it had only been those two items that had been damaged, he should have realized that this was a serious matter.

•

As the media fuss around the incident intensified, Depp refused to budge far from his opening position that there had been an overreaction to what went on in room 1410 that evening. 'I think Johnny obviously has a temper, but this is a very minor incident,' John Waters said of the event. 'The room service must have been bad.' He continued to play it down, telling Depp he 'looked good under arrest'.

Marlon Brando, too, offered his support, but seemed to take the incident more seriously than Waters. So much so, that he phoned Depp's lawyer David Breitbart as soon as he heard news of the arrest. 'He said he was very concerned about Johnny's well-being,' said Breitbart, 'and if there was anything he could do to help, he would like to.' As one wag commented, when you are receiving anger-management advice from Marlon Brando, it is time to take a long hard look at yourself.

Despite Brando's concern, it was more Depp's physical health than his emotional well-being that was a genuine cause for concern at this point. After nine months of not drinking Depp had begun to drink alcohol once more. This led to a decline in the standard of his living in general, which then culminated in a scary episode. 'I was living on coffee and cigarettes,' Depp later explained. 'No food, no sleep. I was sitting around with some pals when my heart started running at two hundred beats a minute.' He was taken to hospital where the treatment administered to him was helpful but brutal. 'I got a shot, boom! A shot that basically stops your heart for a second – now there's an experience that will scare you into shape.'

With the emotional and physical roller coaster he had been riding in recent years, perhaps it was inevitable that he would crack at some point. Had it happened at home, rather than a hotel, perhaps no one would ever have found out about it.

However, there was no chance of privacy and nowhere for Depp to hide as the hotel incident became a leading part of his story, raised whenever he granted press interviews to promote a film. 'I brutalized a hotel room,' he admitted in an interview with David Letterman. When Letterman asked him what led to it, Depp was cagey. 'Bad day,' he said. 'You know, just a bad day.' The host then pointed out that many people have bad days, yet nobody ever *needs* to destroy a hotel room, to which Depp responded: 'How do you know . . . your day may be coming.'

Later, he expanded a little. 'Very simply, I had a bad day,' he said in 2004, with the benefit of ten years' perspective to put the evening into context in his own mind. 'I'd been chased by paparazzi and felt a little bit like novelty boy.' He added: 'I lost it. It was the culmination of many things, a bad spark, and I went off. I did what I felt was necessary. Thank God it wasn't a human being but a hotel room that I took it out on! It was a weird incident. There was a hotel security guard, who was really kind of pissy and arrogant – I wanted to pop him. But I knew that if I did it would obviously be a horse of a different colour: lawsuits and God knows what else. I did my business and they came up to the room. By that point I had cooled down. I said, "I'll of course pay for any damages, I apologize." That wasn't enough. The guy got snooty and shitty. The next thing you know, the police were at the door.'

While everyone can sympathize with somebody who has had a bad day, and all would agree that it would be preferable that Depp took his anger out on a hotel room, rather than another person, his disdain for the security guard is harder to swallow. Depp could not have reasonably expected the hotel to take him at his word that he would pay for the damage and leave the matter there. Quite naturally, the hotel management would have been concerned for Kate Moss's safety and also keen to prevent any further damage to its property. In the circumstances, calling the police was quite understandable. It was only to be expected.

Furthermore, Depp does himself few favours by saying that it was only the fear of a lawsuit that prevented him from hitting the security guard, who he has also accused of 'probably having too many cups of coffee that night'. Having destroyed a hotel room, he was on weak ground in trying to paint anyone else as tetchy. He later returned to his theme that he should have been able to pay for the damages and leave the incident at that. 'I can probably handle the bill,' he said.

It is hard to not feel that many of his pronouncements on the night's events suggested that his wealth or fame should mean he is above the law. Indeed, during his subsequent apologies Depp has also turned a sneer against Roger Daltrey, complaining that, had The Who trashed a hotel room, they would have been 'applauded' for it. 'I was arrested and incarcerated. Age is a wonderful thing, isn't it? Keith Moon [Who drummer and legendary hellraiser] would have been very embarrassed for him. But he was probably used to being embarrassed for him.' The anger is clear, yet he directs it at everyone other than the person responsible for what happened: himself.

However, he was indeed arrested and incarcerated and held for two days at a New York police station. He claimed that while he was there he was given many adoring comments from female police officers. One of them, he said, was less admiring. 'I don't think she likes me,' he said of the odd one out. 'But I bet if she saw me in a mall, she'd ask for my autograph.' Where a period of humility was needed, Depp managed to offer just another moment of arrogance.

His mother was upset to hear of her son's behaviour and arrest. 'She didn't like seeing me in handcuffs on TV, but she knows I'm not a bad person,' said Depp. This is true, and it is worth recalling that this event was an aberration in an otherwise essentially clean track record.

On his release from custody, Depp collected his personal effects from the Mark Hotel and moved to The Carlyle, where he had originally wanted to stay on this trip to New York. As he settled into his favoured venue he might have reflected that had he been able to stay there in the first place, the entire visit might have turned out far more agreeably. Still, the strife was all over and he could now return to normality. Or so he thought. As he picked up his copy of Marlon Brando's memoir, which had been among the possessions he had collected from the Mark Hotel, he was in for a nasty shock. Somebody had scrawled graffiti over several pages of the book. As far as Depp was concerned that 'somebody' had to be a member of staff from the Mark Hotel. The messages ran from 'I hate you' to 'Fuck you, Johnny Depp'. It seemed that somebody was determined to get the last word in.

But let us allow Depp the last word in these pages. As he would later point out, hotels are where he spent a great deal of his time at this stage in his career. Therefore his relationship with, and attitude towards, his hotel room was different to that enjoyed by people who might only spend a week or two each summer in a hotel. This perhaps explains why he was so surprised to be arrested. He felt that he was almost 'at home' in his hotel room, and therefore what happened there should not be of any consequence to the law.

He had recently endured another eventful stay in a hotel in England, during which he believed he had seen his first ghost. 'I was staying in this hotel in England, it used to be a hospital, and I saw this evil surgeon who came at me,' he explained. 'And I wasn't asleep and I wasn't under any type of stimulants. I was straight, and it scared me. It was great. I liked it.' Another time, he said, he slept in a Paris hotel room in the very bed that Oscar Wilde had died in. 'I was a little paranoid that I would be buggered by his ghost,' he quipped.

In the aftermath of the Mark Hotel incident, Depp was mistaken if he thought he would get any respite for a bit – the media got wind of the story and naturally went to town on it. 'I found myself on the covers of all the newspapers, as if this incident was of more importance than the invasion of Haiti,' he said. 'Firstly, you should be allowed to be a human being. Secondly, you should be allowed to have emotion, and thirdly, you should be allowed to have a private life.'

•

Celebrity bust-ups in glamorous hotels have always guaranteed merciless media attention, as Amy Winehouse and her ex-partner Blake Fielder-Civil discovered some years later when they had a noisy scrap inside, and then outside, a swish London hotel. The stories and commentary were feverish and excitable, with speculation mounting that this incident marked the end of Depp's romance with Moss. A fortnight later they did their best to quash this speculation by turning up to three events together in one hectic forty-eight-hour period.

The first came in the shape of the premiere of *Ed Wood*. The following day they appeared at a fund-raising festival for the Paediatric Aids Foundation charity. As if they had not already made their point that all was well between them, they then partied the night away at an event Depp himself had organized at the Metronome Club on Broadway in Manhattan. The bash was to celebrate Mickey Rourke's birthday, but the bigger story of the night was Depp and Moss's public intimacy.

Responding directly to the rumours that he had hit Moss during his fit of rage, Depp said these suggestions were 'Complete bullshit'. He is quick to criticize the tabloid press when he feels it has said something wrong about him. However, he is also swift to confess that he loves reading celebrity gossip rags himself.

Showing his characteristic honesty and indicating how keen he is to avoid charges of hypocrisy, he said: 'I'm fascinated by the tabloid press. I mean, if Demi Moore gets diarrhoea, I want to read about it. I'm sorry, but I do. If Schwarzenegger gets a boil on his rear end, I want to read about that too. But the idea that someone would be fascinated with the private life of someone like me who tells fibs for a living, that's pretty fascinating in itself, isn't it?!'

As is often the case, Depp guards himself from accusations of hypocrisy with care. He can, he feels, only attack the worst excesses of the tabloid media if he admits that he enjoys some aspects of it. With that admission under his belt, he feels empowered to let rip at them when he thinks they have done wrong.

One of the many tabloid assumptions that both Depp and Moss would rail against was that she had some sort of eating disorder. How else, people wondered, could she maintain her ultra-thin body? She insisted that she ate as gluttonously as most people, a claim that Depp backed her up on. 'She eats like a champ,' he said. 'She really puts it away. Why punish somebody because they have a good metabolism? It doesn't make any sense.' He has also suggested that those who propagate untrue rumours about celebrities should find a new hobby, his suggestion being 'Masturbation'.

So, in the light of what happened at the Mark Hotel, the aforementioned description of Depp as the 'most gentle soul' alive might be a little wide of the mark. Perhaps Timothy Leary's words that Depp is 'wild and charitable' comes closer. The Mark Hotel trashing has since become part of Depp folklore, and in the eyes of many it has done him no harm at all. Coming as it did in the 1990s, a decade in which laddish behaviour became increasingly popular in some countries, his behaviour was welcomed by many. Furthermore, while his pronouncements on the episode do seem arrogant and graceless on the surface, they could equally be read in other ways. It might have been that he delivered them with tongue firmly in cheek, but that tone has been lost on many.

He was certainly joking when he pretended that the whole kerfuffle had been sparked by a random appearance in his room of 'a really big dachshund'. He had, he joked, merely been trying to catch the imaginary dog and that the ensuing twenty-minute chase around the room had caused all the damage. He later made the story even more entertainingly fanciful when he decided that the fabled creature may not have been a dog, after all. 'It felt like it was an armadillo,' he joked during an interview with film magazine *Empire*. 'It may have been an elephant.'

He remains steadfastly unwilling to roll over and play dead in the face of criticism, which some find pig-headed. But his straightforward shoulder-shrugging could be read as refreshingly honest. So many Hollywood celebrities have constructed such goodie-goodie public personas that the industry has become a bit of a bore. Furthermore, when Hollywood celebrities are caught misbehaving, the onslaught of public contrition from them can be questionable to say the least. Depp misbehaved and refused to flog himself publicly when caught – and this in itself was a breath of fresh air.

Some sections of the media reflected this sort of attitude. Men's magazine *Esquire* said: 'So he dates the world's most beautiful woman, so he trashes the occasional hotel suite . . . deal with it.' In the same

Seen here at the Cannes Film Festival in 1997 with three glamorous women: Depp's then girlfriend Kate Moss, Hollywood legend Lauren Bacall and Liv Tyler.

Johnny and his mother, Betty Sue, at a Hollywood film premiere in 1995.

Johnny's brother, crime novelist Daniel Depp.

Depp was praised for his performance as Donnie Brasco in the film of the same name, a mafia thriller that also starred Al Pacino.

The 1998 film *Fear and Loathing in Las Vegas* became cult classic. Here Depp and the author of the original book, Hunter S. Thompson, are seen outside a Las Vegas bookstore after a signing session.

Johnny receiving his star on the Hollywood Walk of Fame in Los Angeles in November 1999. Seen here with his mother, Betty Sue, his father John and his girlfriend Vanessa Paradis.

Tim Burton was behind the camera again in 1999 for *Sleepy Hollow*, the period horror drama in which Depp played Ichabod Crane.

Sleepy Hollow premiered at Mann's Chinese Theatre in Los Angeles, to which Johnny escorted his girlfriend Vanessa Paradis.

Heart-throb to millions and devastatingly handsome, Johnny models H & M's spring collection in 1999.

Vanessa Paradis and the couple's first child, Lily-Rose, taking a break on the set of *The Man Who Killed Don Quixote*, in Spain in 2000.

Johnny was 'sinfully delicious' in the smash-hit film *Chocolat* (2000), in which he played Romani gypsy Roux.

In *From Hell* (2001) Depp played police inspector Frederick Abberline on the trail of Jack the Ripper.

The rise of Captain Jack Sparrow began in 2003 with the first in the smash-hit series, *Pirates Of The Caribbean: The Curse of the Black Pearl*.

The Pirates Of The Caribbean series has gone from strength to strength. The second film, *Dead Man's Chest* (above) grossed $135.5 million in the first few days of its release in the US in 2006; while *At World's End* (below) became the most successful film of 2007.

On the set of *Charlie and the Chocolate Factory* in 2005 – another box-office hit – with director Tim Burton.

Helena Bonham Carter as Mrs Lovett and Johnny Depp as Sweeney Todd in the film that won Depp a Golden Globe for Best Actor in a Motion Picture Musical or Comedy.

At New York's Museum of Modern Art's tribute to Tim Burton in November 2009, Johnny is seen here with Helena Bonham Carter (Burton's partner), Tim Burton and Danny DeVito.

Despite its negative critical reception, *The Tourist* (2010) was nominated for three Golden Globes, including one for Johnny Depp as Best Actor: Musical or Comedy.

article, Depp once more complained about his lot. He also claimed that the Mark Hotel had benefitted from the story. 'It's good for them,' Depp says. 'Now they can say they have this little bit of history, this ridiculous morsel of history. They can say, "We had Johnny Depp arrested."'

Here, we should consider a wider issue. Depp might be a Hollywood hero, known all over the world, but he is still an ordinary human being inside with all the good and bad points that entails. 'Fuck it, I'm normal and I want to be normal,' he said. 'But somehow, I'm just not allowed to be. Why can't I be human? I have a lot of love inside me, and a lot of anger inside as well. If I love somebody, then I'm going to love them. If I'm angry and I've got to lash out or hit somebody, I'm going to do it and I don't care what the repercussions are.'

His Mark Hotel trashing quickly became a cultural reference point. In the Woody Allen film *Celebrity*, Leonardo DiCaprio's character destroys a hotel suite after an argument with his girlfriend. Mickey Rourke smashed up a suite at New York's Plaza Hotel (not far from the Mark Hotel and also overlooking Central Park) two months after Depp's fit of pique, prompting Nicholas Cage to ask who Rourke thought he was – the next Johnny Depp?

Awkward times for Depp – or were they? When *Live & Kicking* magazine suggested that these were tough times for him, he was having none of it. 'No this is actually a great time for me – one of the best times I've had,' he said firmly. 'I have a girl who I'm in love with, we have a good, solid relationship and we're having a great time. My family's alive, everyone's OK.'

•

Everyone was indeed just fine, particularly Depp as he enjoyed dating one of the world's most glamorous women. As one would expect, he and Moss moved in some glamorous circles, partying alongside rock star Noel Gallagher and Meg Matthews. It was a strong friendship between the actor and musician; Gallagher even invited Depp to contribute a guitar track to one of Oasis's songs on their feverishly-anticipated third album, *Be Here Now*. The track, 'Fade In-Out', is an epic tune about a roller-coaster, which Gallagher described as 'by far the bluesiest thing I have ever written'. Depp's slide guitar solo is one of its charms. 'Johnny is actually one of the best guitarists we've even seen,' said Gallagher. 'That's why we got him to play the slide guitar solo on "Fade In-Out" – because I couldn't play it,' he added in a rare moment of modesty. 'Afterwards, when were rehearsing for the tour, it took me about six months to work it out to see what he was actually playing.'

Depp was naturally very excited and honoured by this musical link-up with Oasis. 'The guys are pals of mine, and I was in the studio when they put down "Fade In-Out", so they let me play lead slide guitar. We did it in one take, too. I gave Noel Gallagher a white guitar as a gift and he often uses it in gigs. You'll know it's mine because it has the letter "P" on it.'

Later, Gallagher wondered whether Depp's presence on the album would prompt teenie-bopping girls to suddenly become interested in Oasis, though they hardly needed any more fans at this stage, the peak of their popularity. 'It's going to be weird how that's perceived, having a Hollywood star on the album,' he said. 'But I'm glad it happened. If he hadn't been around, we'd have had to get some fat old geezer who'd be telling us about how he played with Clapton in '76 and did a slide solo that lasted for fucking months.' Put that way, their temporary hiring of Depp certainly seemed to have a lot of merit.

This was not the only musical collaboration that Depp undertook around this time, and the letter 'P' was central to the other main one. He had formed a band which went by the name of Pee. It had various members at different times, with hedonistic former Pogue and now Popes frontman Shane MacGowan a regular face alongside Depp in the line-up. 'It's an accident that turned out to be a lot of fun,' Depp told

Elle magazine. The band's publicity notices promised tracks with bizarre names such as 'I Save Cigarette Butts' and 'Michael Stipe', with a sound that was, 'irreverent, brash, raw and tough'. With cover versions of 'Dancing Queen' by Abba also being promised, all of the music enriched by Depp's 'liquid guitar', it sounded an intriguing prospect. Here came a reminder that Depp's initial dream had been to become a musician rather than an actor. He was also a regular sidekick of the band The Red Hot Chilli Peppers, with whom he produced a ten-minute film called *Snuff*, which aimed to 'show the way certain substances take effect'.

So already in the early 1990s, Depp was taking breaks from his acting duties to get involved in more and more musical ventures. Then, in the autumn of 1994, he took on a collaboration of a different kind with his hero and friend Shane MacGowan and his newly formed band The Popes. One of their first singles was a blistering track called 'That Woman's Got Me Drinking'. It is an all-time MacGowan classic, in which the lyrics rage against a woman who has, for seven years, spent her man's money, only to become utterly indifferent to him. He is driven to drink, ultimately downing ten bottles of gin as his heartbreak, fury and frustration build. Outside of his songs for The Pogues, this is one of MacGowan's finest ever compositions. For the promotional video for the single, MacGowan thought big and roped in Depp to direct and to play the song's protagonist. Depp, for so long a fan of MacGowan, readily agreed to take on the role.

In the video, Depp performs masterfully. He sits seething and raging in a bar, served drink after drink by the barman, played by MacGowan. Depp's character is also shown fighting with his girlfriend in a public square. The twist comes at the end of the video, when MacGowan is seen walking off hand-in-hand with the woman who has so tormented Depp. It's a fine video, although it was deemed unsuitable for younger viewers by television channels. 'Some people won't broadcast a video with drinking and smoking in it before 10 p.m.,' sighed MacGowan.

Depp made up for this problem by joining MacGowan for some radio promo interviews for the single. When The Popes performed the single on BBC television's *Top of the Pops*, Depp joined them on stage, guaranteeing extra attention and buzz around the song's release. He was introduced on the show as Johnny 'Edward Scissorhands' Depp. He appeared wearing a shirt that he had bought many years earlier, while he was playing with The Kids in Florida.

During a photo shoot for *NME* magazine on the same day, Depp seemed to be enthralled and excited to be alongside MacGowan. After the photographs were taken, he told the interviewer how he had first met his hero and how he regarded him. 'He's a piece of work, isn't he?' he said. 'The first time I met Shane . . . he doesn't remember it. He was on a pool table, guitar in one hand and a bottle of wine in the other. He was tired . . . ha ha ha ha. It wasn't until two years later when I was in Dublin with Gerry [Conlon, of the Guildford Four] that I met Shane. I was always a big fan of The Pogues and I think he's one of the few true poets around. Just hanging out with him was great; when he asked me to come round and play on his record, that was a real honour. Though I guess you could always cover it in the mix if I was shitty, right?'

A journalist witnessed an amusing exchange between MacGowan and his manager which showed that the singer was just as admiring of Depp. 'He's my friend,' the manager told MacGowan. 'So, he was my friend *before* he was your friend,' replied the singer competitively. Given what a grouch he can be, the fact that MacGowan was inclined to speak this way about Depp shows just how fond of him he is.

Protective of him too, for the singer spoke bluntly of the circus of fame that he saw erected around Depp. 'We're mates, but of course now it's turned into a big fucking scene,' he wrote in *Q* magazine. He went on to express his horror at what Depp and he encountered outside the *Top of the Pops* studio. 'Johnny was hounded by photographers, and everybody was trying to get an angle on it – my record company, all the papers. I was more pissed off than he was about it all. There was a whole gang of about twenty or thirty photographers there, all snapping away . . . I thought that was quite bizarre, I must admit, but that was the movie star angle.' This was another instance of an already famous person expressing their surprise at the level of media pressure that Depp had to contend with. Again, this shows that his star had risen far higher than that of other household names.

Interestingly, Depp compared MacGowan to another of his heroes, Marlon Brando. It is not perhaps the most immediate comparison that an outsider would make, but Depp made his case persuasively. 'These are two guys who are completely true to their vision: non-conforming, uncompromising,' he said. 'I think Marlon is an incredibly gifted artist. Beyond the fact that Marlon is considered the most gifted actor of our time, I think he's an artist in his thoughts, ideas and anything he does. Shane's the same. They're a couple of guys whose first instinct is always to go against the grain. It's an admirable trait in anyone.'

MacGowan would make a puzzling comparison between himself and Depp, claiming they were 'both easy-going guys who want a peaceful life but can't get one'. On the face of it, MacGowan's life story seems one of a man who wants anything but a peaceful life.

As for Depp, his life was to be far from peaceful when he decided one evening to take on the paparazzi. Taking a course of action which many celebrities must have fantasized about, he threatened a gang of photographers with physical violence. Looking back in later, calmer days, Depp said: 'I haven't had much of a problem since I threatened them with a piece of wood'. Taking up the story, he explained: 'I was coming out of this restaurant, and I said politely, "I really don't want to be a showboat. I don't want to be that guy tonight." They weren't going for it. So I grabbed the wood. I look at it as a scientific experiment in human behaviour. And the unfortunate result that I came up with that night is that violence works. Since then, they've been OK and left me alone.'

It had been a memorable evening for Depp, the photographers, the restaurant owners and the police. All of them became the players in this confrontational evening in which Depp's years of bubbling frustration with the media boiled over.

Realizing the paparazzi were not going to leave him alone, despite his requests, he picked up the aforementioned piece of wood. 'I guess the restaurant use it as a door jamb,' he said. 'I picked it up and . . . er . . . smacked one of them on the hand with it and I went outside and I said: "Now. Please. Take my picture. Please. Because the first one, the first flash that I see, is the recipient of this. Let's have it. Let's do it. Let's have our photo shoot."'

He went on to explain that for the next ten minutes, the photographers were suddenly bashful and not a single flash went off. Then, the police arrived and suddenly the flashes began again. Depp was arrested – not his finest hour but one that he has never admitted to regretting at all. 'But it was in fact a beautiful moment,' he said. 'It was a beautiful moment because it showed them for what they really are. And there was a kind of poetry to it. It was beautiful. I don't regret it at all. I mean, if I had to do it again, that kind of thing, I would do it again.' He insisted that even during his five hours in custody he did not regret taking a stand. Indeed, he was kept entertained during his incarceration by the fact that British police cells are called 'custody suites', which he found amusing.

●

In January 1995, Moss had a milestone birthday. As she turned twenty-one, Depp put on a special bash for her. It was held in familiar surroundings of The Viper Room, but it was no ordinary evening. Here we see Depp's romantic and thoughtful side. 'They opened the curtains and there was my mum, my dad and everyone had flown in from London and New York,' remembered

Kate with delight. 'And John Galliano had come from Paris. It was amazing. I was ... shaking ... I had to go into the office for ten minutes till I'd calmed down.'

No sooner had she emerged than she was trembling again. Depp had booked Gloria Gaynor and Thelma Houston to sing 'Happy Birthday' to her. As Gaynor sang, 'Happy birthday, Miss Moss' the birthday girl felt, quite naturally, like she was in heaven.

But would Depp and Moss take the relationship to the next level and marry? When he splashed out over $2 million on a new home, it prompted speculation both ways. Some said the purchase was a precursor to Depp and Moss tying the knot and starting a family, others suggested that this move was to lead straight to their split. For the time being, neither speculation would prove true. However, it was a fine property. The mansion, originally named The Castle, was near the Sunset Strip and set in two and a half acres of private grounds. 'I just love the house,' said Depp. 'It's such a strange design, very unusual architecture. It's like a weird little castle in the middle of Hollywood'. He added that though he was rarely in town to enjoy the place, he employed a housekeeper known as Mr Pink to keep it all running.

This house was a love nest for Depp and Moss at times, but that did not mean it was about to become a marital home, as they were quick to point out, amid speculation to the contrary. 'He's just my boyfriend, we're not getting married,' said Moss. Depp echoed this statement, saying that though he loved Moss enough to marry her, 'as far as putting our names on paper, making weird public vows that signify ownership, that's not on the cards'.

Meanwhile, back on the big screen, Depp starred in a new film, *Don Juan DeMarco*, directed by Jeremy Leven. A medium-budget romantic comedy, the film follows a man who believed himself to be the legendary lover and libertine Don Juan. Leven could not believe that nobody had made a film around Don Juan's character before, so he decided to make one himself. In his film, the lead character undergoes psychiatric treatment to try and rid him of his delusions, and it is this character that Leven wanted Depp to play. Given his Cherokee roots, Depp has a look that lends itself well to playing Latin characters. His response was that he would take the part on one condition: that his hero Marlon Brando play the part of the shrink who treats him. This was not a challenge as such, for Depp was willing to convince Brando himself, provided Leven gave him the go-ahead, which he did.

So Depp picked up the phone and, with a little trepidation, called Brando. The legend was polite and down to earth with Depp. He invited him to dinner to discuss the proposition. Over a somewhat unlikely evening meal of take-away Chinese food, the two Hollywood stars talked over the film and what they could bring to their respective roles. Eventually Brando agreed to take on the part. This was immensely exciting news for Depp, who would now be working alongside one of his all-time heroes. He had played guitar with Oasis and worked alongside Shane MacGowan, but for Depp this was an even bigger deal.

It was a massive deal for the film, too. Originally Leven had envisaged a $3 million budget for his project, but it was now working to a budget of over $20 million. The other immediate effect of Brando coming on board was that it became far easier to convince other big names to follow suit – and at a fraction of their usual price. Faye Dunaway was one of the stars that signed up, in her case to play Brando's character's wife.

Meanwhile, Depp was researching his role. One of the things that occurred to him as he did was that, unlike Don Juan, he himself actually had relatively modest experience sexually, certainly when it came to sheer quantity of partners. However, when it came to filming Depp was as magisterial as ever. He reportedly perfected the Latino accent required by watching reruns of the television series *Fantasy Island*. He performed with passion and authenticity and, as his co-stars and the crew were quick to realize, he and Brando had a great rapport. The director watched them act out a scene in which Depp had to let his eyes partially, but not fully, fill with tears. Depp pulled off the trick, and Brando said of the moment: 'That kid is great'.

To hell with the words of the critics whether positive or damning – this was the sort of feedback that Depp lived for. Having been so in awe of Brando for so long, and having studied and admired his acting ability, to receive such a warm verdict from his hero was an astonishing boost to Johnny's confidence. Not least because Brando is not one to insincerely throw praise around wherever he went. Quite the contrary, in fact. This was the real thing.

'Brando adores [Depp],' noticed Dunaway. 'He loves Johnny's genuineness and modesty and that he is who he is . . . [Brando] knows how to recognize a sham in any shape.' Naturally, Depp felt just as happy about Brando. 'Working with Marlon is the greatest thing that's happened in my life,' he said. 'I mean, where do you go from here? Who would have thought? Marlon is not a myth; he's everything people think he is.' He added that, although Brando was at this stage in his seventies, he was more akin to 'a child genius' than an old man.

Brando's praise made the thoughts of the critics almost irrelevant to Depp, but for the record, the reaction to *Don Juan DeMarco* was mostly very positive. *Empire* magazine was so impressed with Depp's performance that it concluded he had been born to play the character. *The Guardian* made the exact same point, but the passage that would have meant most to Depp was their conclusion that he 'stood up to Brando as the best young actor in Hollywood'. *Variety* magazine wrote that 'heavily accented Depp is delightfully fetching. Meanwhile, Peter Travers, in the *Washington Post*, said that it was this pairing that stopped it becoming a 'forgettable' film. 'What jump-starts the film is the casting of Johnny Depp as Don Juan and Marlon Brando as his shrink. They bring a playfully romantic touch to a drama that could have been dead weight in clumsier hands.' His conclusion placed Depp once more on the level of his hero. 'Depp ranks with the best actors of his generation. Near the end of the film he pierces the heart by revealing the lost boy beneath the macho bravado. It's an art that Brando mastered in the days of *A Streetcar Named Desire* and *On the Waterfront*.'

As for Depp, his next film was a Western, and here his pairing with the director promised to be a fascinating and unconventional affair that could result in something glorious, or just as easily end in something close to disaster. Jim Jarmusch was one of the leading lights of independent and cult cinema throughout the 1980s and by the time he worked with Depp in the 1990s, he was still ruling that particular roost. Among his films were *Stranger Than Paradise*, and *Down By Law*, which starred

Depp's musical hero Tom Waits. He and Depp were also good friends, so when he asked Depp to take part in what he was calling an 'Acid Western' he was to make called *Dead Man*, he got a positive response. Jarmusch had long noted a contrast between Depp professionally and personally. 'In real life, sometimes, it's hard for him to decide where to eat or what to do,' said the director, 'but as an actor he's very precise.'

Indeed, given how non-commercial and downright strange the movie was to be, it was just right for Depp. The cast collected together a glorious band of talented oddballs including rock legend Iggy Pop, gravelly-voiced and wild-living British acting legend John Hurt, and – in what turned out to be his final role – noir legend, Robert Mitchum. As for Depp, his part was as William Blake, an accountant who becomes an unlikely outlaw in the nineteenth-century Wild West. 'I wrote this film with Johnny Depp in my head for the character of Blake,' said Jarmusch. He added that, had Depp not agreed to appear, then he might never have made the film. Fortunately Depp did sign up – and at a very early stage in the planning. That helped Jarmusch, particularly because the movie had so much about it that could potentially put off movie houses, including the fact he insisted he would shoot it in black and white.

'What I love about Johnny for this character,' commented Jarmusch, 'is that he has the ability to start off very innocently. This is a difficult role to play, to start off as a passive character in a genre that is based on active, aggressive central characters.' He added that Depp effortlessly went through 'a lot of very subtle but big changes in his character'.

Jarmusch also expressed surprise at just how 'precise and inventive' Depp proved as an actor. The film turned into a very offbeat affair and was, in the opinion of many viewers and critics, rather hard work to watch. If anything, the reviewers tended to be baffled. The *Chicago Sun Times's* Roger Ebert wrote: 'Jim Jarmusch is trying to get at something here, and I don't have a clue what it is'. However, a *New York Times* critic later named it 'one of the very best movies of the 1990s'.

One incident during filming reminded Johnny once again of the price of fame. He later explained what happened to a journalist from *Playboy* magazine. 'I was hanging out with Jarmusch and the crew, smoking cigarettes, and there was a guy lurking, checking me out,' he began. 'He looked normal enough, but his eyes were a little too open. So I knew he'd come up to me, which he did. "Hi, Johnny! Wanna go have a drink?" I said, "Thanks, I'm OK." He said, "Listen, you could really help me out. My wife and I are separating, but I want to get back with her. She's a big fan of yours." He wanted me to go home with him and mediate his divorce. I wouldn't, so he said he'd call her on the phone and we could talk it out. Now, that stuff goes too far. You want to say, "Can't we just kiss? Could you just shove your tongue down my gullet and be done with it?"'

•

Away from work, Depp was still having to fend off questions about whether he and Moss planned to marry one day. In reality it barely mattered whether marriage was on the cards or not, the media continued to be obsessed with Depp and Moss's relationship.

In January 1996, Depp again arranged something special for his girlfriend's birthday. They had a fine meal at a top London restaurant, but it is what is rumoured to have happened back at their hotel that has become of more interest to the public. Depp and Moss dispute the legend that has grown around events at the hotel, but what a legend it is. They were staying at the Portobello Hotel, a fine, neo-classical mansion that stands grandly, but quietly, on a Notting Hill street. Since opening in 1971, it has built a reputation as a perfect place to hide from the world. It's no wonder that Depp was keen on the place after all, this is the venue that *Newsweek* magazine described as one that 'happily flaunts its own eccentricity'.

The story goes that while staying in Room 13, Depp

and Moss asked for the bath tub to be filled with champagne. It was alleged to have taken three cases of bubbly to fill the tub. Naurally, news of this extravagant arrangement became the source of much chatter in the media. When it was also alleged that, while the couple were out having dinner, a maid emptied the bath tub because she assumed it was full of cold water, the story became too much for any gossipmonger to resist. The hotel confirmed that 'a couple' had indeed made such a request, but refused to confirm it was Depp and Moss. 'They saw the fun side,' said Johnny Ekperigin, managing partner of the hotel, when asked what the couple's reaction was when they learned the bath had been drained. 'When you earn over £20 million a year it does not really matter, does it?'

The hotel has since used the story as a marketing tool. So have the makers of a 'champagne-flavoured' bubble bath product, the advertisement for which invites users to bathe like Johnny Depp and Kate Moss. But is the story true? Despite the Portobello Hotel's hint that the couple involved in the story were 'an American actor and English model', Depp flatly denies it. 'I wish it was true,' he said. The story refuses to die, though at least as far as contested tabloid legends go, this one is fairly harmless.

Johnny's next part was in a film with a tantalizing plot, just what film critics delighted in describing as 'edge-of-your-seat' stuff. Directed by John Badham, *Nick of Time* saw Depp appear as Gene Watson, a widowed Californian accountant. His six-year-old daughter is kidnapped and Watson is handed a gun and a photograph of a woman and told that unless he kills her in the next seventy-five minutes, he will never see his daughter again. The film continues in 'real time' giving it even more excitement and nervy drama. As a member of the crew commented, this role was one that stood in contrast to the offbeat outsiders Depp had become associated with.

His character was an everyday, placid man thrown into a horrific dilemma that, though outlandish, was one that audiences could nevertheless relate to. Given that during the film Depp had to take part in some mainstream action movie scenes, *Nick of Time* could be said to have come along at just the right point to save Depp from being typecast. With this film, therefore, we see him move into a new, third phase in his acting career. He began as a teenage idol, then furiously distanced himself from that image by playing outsiders in quirky films. Having made his point, he was now ready to return towards the mainstream again – but only on his own terms, as always.

Cynics were quick to line up and swipe at him, accusing him of 'doing a Keanu' – shorthand for selling out. Depp was immune to these suggestions. 'Who cares? I'm interested in story and character and doing things that haven't been done a zillion times. When I read *Nick of Time* I could see the guy mowing the grass, watering his lawn, putting out the Water Wiggle in the backyard for his kid, and I liked the challenge of playing him. He's nothing like me.'

Although he was yet to become a father at this stage, Depp could tap deep into his character's feelings. 'I drew on what was accessible,' he said, adding that he had nieces and nephews of whom he was so fond that he could imagine a parent's feelings too. He reminded us again that 'family is very important to me', still seemingly trying to reconcile in his own mind the break-up of his parents when he was a child.

The film, also starring Christopher Walken, was shot with a naturalistic bent, almost more akin to a real-life documentary than a movie. For instance, the scenes were shot in chronological order, something that is rarely the case with modern movies. Also, because up to three cameras were used for several scenes, which lessened the usual strict positioning pressure, Depp felt liberated as he acted. Often handheld cameras were used, which only increased the tension. The director was pleased with his lead's performance, even though he noticed that Depp often arrived on set in downtown Los Angeles looking a little the worse for the wear, having apparently partied the night before. 'What I learned right away was, it didn't matter if he never went to bed the night before, because he was right on top of it,' said Badham, explaining why he did not mind.

The *Sunday Telegraph* reviewer Anne Billson did not think that Depp played the role of an ordinary Joe convincingly, in part for reasons that were not under his control. 'Depp's attempts to impersonate an average Joe aren't entirely convincing – he's way too good looking,' she wrote. Indeed, the critical reception was largely unimpressed, with *Rolling Stone* magazine concluding: 'A movie in which time is of the essence is really a botch job when you don't believe a minute of it.' At least *Variety* magazine was more positive, taking the opposite stance to the *Sunday Telegraph*: 'Depp tries his hand at an every-day Joe with solid results,' wrote Brian Lowry. Whatever the critics thought, Depp took encouragement from this part; it reminding him that he was a multi-faceted artist.

The next project that he signed up for promised so much: the chance to reunite on screen with Marlon Brando, an enjoyable eight-week shoot in Ireland and much more. So it was with excitement that Depp began work, playing the part of an investigative journalist, in the film *Divine Rapture*. However, around a quarter of the way through filming, the movie makers dropped a bombshell: the funding for the film had been withdrawn and the project was cancelled. Depp, Brando and the rest of the cast and crew had been having a ball. No wonder they were so disappointed at having to walk away from the project, though at least in his disappointment Depp came up with a memorable quote. 'It was like being in the middle of good sex and then having the lights turn on and fifteen people with machine guns come in and say, "Stop or die",' he said of this enforced cinematic coitus interruptus.

Speaking of matters carnal, Depp had become the envy of men across the world with his relationship with Kate Moss. However, the end of that relationship was not far away, as yet another attempt by the actor to attain domestic bliss went by the wayside. Although no official reasons have been given for the split, speculation had it that his keenness for the couple to start a family was a significant contributory factor. Depp being the man he was, it was not long before he was dating another beautiful, famous woman. This time, though, the relationship would have longevity.

CHAPTER SIX:

BECOMING A LEGEND

Depp's directorial debut should have been a proud and exciting experience for him, as he added another string to his professional bow. With this move, he could really imprint his creativity and vision onto a film, in a way that was not possible when merely an actor in a movie. Although he derived pleasure and satisfaction from the experience, however, it proved to be fraught with a far higher degree of challenge than Depp had ever imagined.

The film in question was called *The Brave*. He explained the premise of the movie in an interview with *Elle* magazine. 'It's a strange story about a Native American and his family, living in a desert shanty town in abject poverty,' he said. 'One day the young Indian is presented with an opportunity to make enough money to save his family. He is offered a part in a "snuff" film in which he would sacrifice his life. Will he, or won't he? It's an interesting situation and there are a lot of parallels to the atrocities that were committed against Native Americans a century ago.' Given that the subject of the film was one that was sensitive in America, Depp was making his first stab as a director in uncommercial territory. Consequently, it was a challenge to raise funding and other backing for his project.

However, none other than Marlon Brando came to the rescue. Depp's hero, sometime co-star and friend came on board as a cast member and his presence, together with that of Depp among the cast as well as crew, pushed a previously meagre budget up to $7 million. 'For Marlon to come in and do this part for me was one of the greatest gifts I've ever been given in my life,' said a delighted, relieved Depp. It was game on!

Putting aside the specific framework of the Native American story, the basic premise of the plot of *The Brave* was very Depp. His love of family and fascination with the concept of parents who are willing to go through a sacrifice on behalf of their children are strong. Indeed, this film marked a less commercial take on the theme of *Nick of Time*. However, while he had greatly enjoyed appearing in that film, his work on *The Brave* was to test his patience almost to the limit.

Although Depp was grateful for Brando's presence, who he said helped enormously as 'a friend, an actor and as a director,' he was taken by surprise by just what an increase in work his ascension to the latter role would entail. As he slogged away at the film for up to eighteen hours each day, Depp grew exhausted physically and overwhelmed mentally by the scale of the project. He had not expected it to be so tough and all-consuming. Furthermore, the dual roles of director and actor meant that he was regularly forced to do something he never enjoyed: watching himself on screen. 'It's the most insane thing I have ever done,' he reflected later.

Thankfully, Brando's support and humour made

the testing times more fun – Depp remembers them 'cackling and laughing' together as they worked. He was also pleased to find that he did not have to direct Brando, as he was nailing every scene without any direction needed. The movie legend pleased Depp by going 'above and beyond anything I ever expected' in his efforts on set. 'He really dug inside,' purred Depp.

The critics were not so kind when they assessed Depp's directorial debut. *Time Out* magazine was typical when it said: 'Besides the implausibilities, the direction has two fatal flaws: it's both tediously slow and hugely narcissistic as the camera focuses repeatedly on Depp's bandanna'd head and rippling torso.'

Elsewhere, it was called 'morbid' and one critic wrote that there was 'a lot wrong' with the film. *Variety* magazine called the film 'turgid and unbelievable'. At least *The Guardian*'s Jonathan Romney said that Depp 'should be encouraged' to try directing again. Of far more impact than any of these words on the confidence of 'director Depp', though, was the standing ovation it received at the Cannes Film Festival in May 1997. The respect of his peers is always of far more importance.

The longer his career went on, the more film legends Depp appeared with on screen. During the mid-1990s he appeared in a fine gangster film called *Donnie Brasco*, alongside one of cinema's most legendary gangster-actors: Al Pacino. Director Mike Newell explained that

Depp was drawn to the role because the character had to 'run beneath the surface'. Expanding on what he meant by this, Newell added: 'Johnny is one of those actors who acts in a kind of long term. You stay with his characterizations throughout a film because he tells you his story in his own good time. And more important, you are willing to wait for it.' Newell also noted that Depp is 'a great impersonator'. The director was able to study this at close range, because to perfect his part for the film, Depp spent time with the man he was portraying in it – Joe Pistone, a.k.a. Donni Brasco.

Pistone was an FBI agent who worked undercover for several years, infiltrating the New York mafia family under the 'Brasco' identity. His work led to the conviction of over a hundred mafia men, guaranteeing him legendary status in the annals of crime history, not to mention earning him hundreds of bitter enemies.

Newell was present when Depp first met Pistone (who lives under a secret identity), and he recalled with vividness the actor's powers of observation and mimicry. 'I could see him latch on to certain characteristics in seconds,' recalled the director. 'Joe is a man whose exterior is stony . . . I would not want to get beaten up by Joe, truly.' So Depp would tread carefully when it came to mimicking Pistone's mannerisms.

Fortunately, his portrayal received the seal of approval from the man himself, who said that Depp had 'captured me to a tee'. He added that Depp had an astonishing memory, explaining, 'he's like a sponge'. It had been a careful study from the sponge, who even went as far as phoning Pistone's wife with questions about her husband, all the better to nail him on screen. Actor and subject hit it off well, even working out in the gym together on a few occasions.

Depp also built up a great rapport with his co-star, the sensationally talented Al Pacino. He described working with the *Godfather* legend as 'a real treat and an honour'. He had expected Pacino to be a very serious chap, but actually found, to his delight, that he was 'very loose and playful . . . constantly making jokes and making people laugh'.

To Depp's childlike delight, Pacino shared his long-standing amusement with flatulence. As they prepared to start work one day, Depp and Pacino were sitting together in a car when suddenly a 'huge ripping fart' sound emerged from Depp's direction, Newell explained. Depp apologized, but then a few seconds later a second such sound emerged. Pacino, understandably, opened the car window. Then came a third fart noise, at which point Pacino gave Depp a confused stare. Depp then revealed that the noises had been coming not from his bowels, but from a whoopee cushion. Far from disapproving of such immaturity, Pacino thought that 'that was the greatest thing since sliced bread'.

The film, much of which was filmed in Depp's childhood state of Florida, was nominated for an Academy Award for Best Adapted Screenplay. It . received admiring write-ups, with Depp described as 'sensational' by one critic and 'graceful' by another. It was Pacino, however, who received the loudest cheers, with *Entertainment Weekly* qualifying its praise for Depp by declaring: 'If *Donnie Brasco* belongs to any actor, though, it's Al Pacino.'

For Depp, working with Pacino had been an enjoyable experience, and it was also a relief to be back solely as an actor on a film, rather than also juggling directorial duties. Indeed his previous directorial duties had had an unfortunate effect on his life away from work. With his long hours and consequent exhaustion he was rarely there for Kate – physically or emotionally.

Whether they knew it or not, their relationship was nearing its end, but there was one more amazing experience for them to share, an experience that would bring Depp face to face with another of his idols, something he was increasingly enjoying.

Hunter S. Thompson was a legendary journalist and author – but he was so much more than that. Born in Kentucky in the 1930s, Thompson was a rebellious man throughout his adult life. Indeed, before he had even left school he had served thirty days' juvenile detention for some childish misdeeds. On joining the military it was only a matter of time before he was thrown out. Fortunately his easy charm was such that, despite his misbehaviour, he got off with nothing more than an honourable discharge.

He was drawn towards writing as a profession, but was again on the margins of it. He enjoyed drug-taking, hanging out with Hell's Angels and then writing about the inevitable scrapes in which he found himself. One of his first books was called *The Rum Diary*, but the work that would make him an icon was *Fear and Loathing in Las Vegas*, which first appeared over two instalments in *Rolling Stone* magazine and was then published as a book. It was this book that launched 'gonzo journalism', a first-person style of writing in which the journalist was a key figure in the unfolding action. This style was also frequently associated with hedonism, something Thompson knew a great deal about.

Off the back of the success of that book Thompson became an icon, his wild ways celebrated by admirers across the world. The dangerous side to his personality only served to attract more admiration, which in turn served to encourage him in his drinking, drug-taking and gun-wielding ways. He lived a mystical life in Colorado, where Depp first met him, before he even knew he was to later to portray him on the big screen. It was over the Christmas period of 1995 and Depp was holidaying nearby with Moss, and her mother and brother. They met Thompson at his local bar. What sort of evening did it turn into? 'The whole evening, I will never forget it,' remembered Moss. 'It was just so mad. My mum being there, the bomb.'

That was the sort of evening it turned into. Depp and his crew were drinking in the Woody Creek Tavern, a bar that became synonymous with Thompson. Indeed, they went there hoping to meet Thompson, but for some time there was no sign of the notorious regular. Then, late into the night, he appeared. As Depp recalled, Thompson had, 'a "taser" gun in his left hand and a huge cattle prod in his right hand, swinging them around getting people to move out of his way'. It was quite an entrance, but a relatively serene moment when compared with what was to come.

Although Depp idolized Thompson, the writer was scarcely aware of Depp's existence. However, as Depp told him, they both had heritage in Kentucky, so Thompson joined Depp's group. Drinks were drunk, words and laughter exchanged. After plenty of all three, Thompson decided he liked Depp, and invited the group back to his home for more liquid refreshment.

As Thompson showed Depp around his ranch, Depp was particularly impressed by a gun that was set on the wall. So Thompson handed him the gun, and they walked to the kitchen. In the kitchen ingredients were laid out, not to make a fine meal, but to make an almighty explosion. 'He had a couple of big tanks of propane in there and handed me some nitroglycerine capsules,' said Depp. 'We taped them to the side of the tank, took it out back, and I shot it. I've shot guns since I was eight years old, so I knew I could hit something.' When the bullet Depp fired connected with the explosive target, the results were spectacular. 'Boof! Bullseye!' said Depp. 'There was this seventy-five foot burst of fire, an enormous explosion.' As he also acknowledged, it was fortunate that nobody was hit by the explosion or the shrapnel that it projected so widely. 'Mrs Moss was a little freaked out,' he said of his girlfriend's mother. 'But she did well. She hung in there.' After they left Thompson's ranch, Mrs Moss turned to Depp and asked who exactly their strange host was.

Two years later, Depp was to portray their strange host on the big screen. He was hired to play the part of Raoul Duke (Thompson's character) in the film adaptation of *Fear and Loathing in Las Vegas*. Therefore, his brush with Thompson was to prove the first step in some expert research for a part Depp was beyond excited to be taking on. His next step was to move into the aforementioned ranch to try his hand at living like Thompson. 'I was blessed enough, or cursed enough, to spend a good three or four months with Hunter Thompson prior to filming,' said Depp at a Cannes press conference. Sleeping in the basement, with his makeshift bed next to a big vat of gunpowder, even his sleeping hours were hard work. He had not realized for the first five days that he was sleeping next to a store of gunpowder – but once he did, he stopped smoking in bed.

For Depp, though, going the extra mile for the part was certainly worthwhile. 'I felt under tremendous pressure – I was so freaked out by the idea of disappointing Hunter,' he said. 'So I did my best to absorb him. My goal was to steal his soul. That's what I wanted to do, to try and take as much of him as possible and put him into my body.'

To that end, he also pored over Thompson's notebooks. Living the dream of fans of the writer from across the globe, he was able to connect very strongly with the man and his mind. On occasion, Thompson would sit and listen as Depp read aloud from the books. The writer admired how closely the actor mimicked his delivery, and corrected him where he had it wrong. All the while, Depp was observing Thompson's mannerisms and noting them down in his head. 'I know it sounds really goofy and all that stuff,' he said, 'but I felt like him, especially when we were doing it. I found it hard to find Johnny in a way because I felt more like Hunter. Even when I was not working, at the weekends, I felt like Hunter.'

Given that he had previously spoken with disapproval of the thespians who get so absorbed in method acting that they remain in character even off set, this was a new feeling for him. So much so, that on reflection later he wondered whether he had overdone it. 'It has gone too deep, it really has,' he said, seemingly in jest, but perhaps with a least a kernel of seriousness.

To play the part, Johnny also had to have his famous long head of hair shaved off. Although this meant a drastic change in his appearance, he had long been resigned to the need for it. 'I believe the decision to shave my head, you know, and keep this little horseshoe of fuzz around the edge was ... I knew I was going to have to do that right away as soon as we started to dive in,' he said in Cannes.

He denied that the film glorified drug use. 'Absolutely not, I mean when you see this film and you see what these guys ingest, and then feel, and go through, and then expel from their being, it's not like I watch it and go, "Jesus, what a great idea! Let's get really high and puke!" or "I'd love to see people wandering around with six hairy tits on their back".' Rather than an advert for drug use, said Depp, the film was instead 'like a drug nightmare'. Therefore, he argued, his part in such a film did not contradict the anti-drug message he had championed in the past, including in the form of the short film he directed in the wake of River Phoenix's death.

The *New York Times* felt that *Fear and Loathing in Las Vegas* was 'clumsily anchored' by Depp's narration and that, furthermore, that made it 'fall flat'. Elsewhere, the *San Francisco Chronicle* noted that Depp's intensive study of Thompson's mannerisms had paid off, but felt that 'underneath all his buggy gestures and tics, he doesn't show us a personality'. *USA Today*'s review was even more damning, describing the film as 'simply unwatchable', while in Britain *The Guardian* complained that 'there's an element of tedium' to the production.

In time, it was to attract more happy reviews, such as when *Empire* magazine placed it at 469 in its '500 Greatest Movies of All Time' list. Depp also won a Golden Aries Award from the Russian Guild of Film Critics for his part in the film. Not the most prestigious of gongs by any means, but an award all the same.

However, for Depp perhaps the critical outcome of his part in the film was that, once again, people spoke of the fact he was playing an outsider character again. Commentators' ability to never tire of making that observation is astonishing. However, more mainstream roles were not far away for him.

•

In the meantime, it was becoming increasingly clear to him and Moss that their relationship was doomed. For some time the media had been speculating that they had split. Although much of this speculation was incorrect in strict factual terms, in spirit it was close to the truth. The media was following their every footstep during 1997 and 1998 as they partied with the Rolling Stones for her birthday, and reportedly moved in together first in New York City and then in Paris.

It was in France, at the Cannes Film Festival in May 1998, that the world saw them together for the last time. Just days later, they officially announced that they had split. 'Kate is somebody I care deeply about,' said Depp as their four-year relationship came to an end, describing her as 'a great, lovely, sweet, pure girl'. He mourned the fact that he had not given her the level of attention she deserved. 'I let my career get in the way,' he sighed. 'I've just been very stupid . . . Trust me, I'm a total moron at times.' This willingness to blame himself for the break-up had a slice of chivalry to it, one that is not entirely commonplace among famous men.

He never responded to suspicions that the break-up was the result of Moss not sharing his desire to start a family together, but he did confirm that this remained a fond aspiration of his. 'I want to have children, he said. 'I'd really like to become a parent now, but finding the right woman to share that with is proving difficult.' As fate would have it, he had already briefly met the woman who would have his children. But it was only upon a later encounter with her that they connected.

In the summer of 1998, he travelled to France to

appear in a Roman Polanski film called *The Ninth Gate*. It turned out to be an important journey, the results of which changed his life forever and continue to influence it to this very day. 'I came over here to make a movie,' he said, '[but I also] met a girl, got a place, had a baby.'

The Ninth Gate was an unconventional movie about, of all things, a rare book dealer. Depp played the dealer, Dean Corso, who, while searching out the two remaining copies of a rare tome, becomes embroiled in a conspiracy with supernatural dimension. Combining elements of the classic mystery movie genre with others, including neo-noir, the film was in danger of becoming overindulgent from the start.

A previous supernatural film from Polanski, 1968's *Rosemary's Baby*, had become so popular among film-buffs that, for many people, his new film with that same flavour was always going to be a tough sell. The critics savaged it, with the *Village Voice*'s verdict that *The Ninth Gate* was 'barely releasable hokum, stuffed with cheesy blah-blah', a far from uncommon consensus. At least the *San Francisco Chronicle* said that 'Depp is the best reason to see Polanski's satanic thriller'.

However, the most profound legacy of his trip to France had nothing to do with the film. Instead, it came from his meeting with French singer, model and actress Vanessa Paradis. Born near Paris in December 1972, Paradis is among the most glamorous French stars of recent times. By the time she was fourteen she was a child star, having appeared on television and released a single. However, it was not until she released her second single, 'Joe Le Taxi' that she became globally famous. The video of a glamorous mid-teen Paradis was like a forerunner to that created for the Britney Spears hit, 'Baby One More Time'. She became an idol to girls across the globe, and an object of desire for teenage boys. In the 1990s, as well as continuing with her musical career, Vanessa also modelled for companies such as Chanel. Later, in the 1990s she became more involved in acting, including a part opposite Gérard Depardieu in a crime thriller, *Élisa*.

While in France shooting *The Ninth Gate*, Depp met Paradis properly, but there had been a brief, passing encounter prior to that. 'We met briefly years ago,' he said. 'I remember thinking "Ouch", it was just hello, but the contact was electric.' That had been five years previously. On the second occasion, he was in the reception of his hotel, collecting some messages from the receptionist when he turned round and saw Paradis again. 'She had on a dress with an exposed back,' he recalled. 'I thought, "Wow!" Suddenly, the back turned and she looked at me. I walked right over, and there were those eyes again – I knew it was her. She asked, "Do you remember me?"' Depp confirmed that indeed he did, and invited her to have a drink with him.

As they sat and talked, he was, not for the first time in his life, struck by an instant certainty that he had found the woman for him. 'It was over with at that point,' he said in an interview for *New Idea* magazine. 'I knew I was in big trouble.' He added: 'I pretty much fell in love with Vanessa the moment I set eyes on her. As a person I was pretty much a lost cause at that point of my life. She turned all that around for me with her incredible tenderness and understanding. She made me feel like a real human being again, instead of someone Hollywood had manufactured. It sounds incredibly corny and phoney, but that's exactly what happened to me and what she has meant to me.'

If Depp's words make it sound as though he and Paradis became very serious very quickly, then that's because they really did. In the latter stages of his relationship with Moss, Depp had hardly seen his erstwhile partner. With Paradis, he was keen to not make that mistake again. During the summer months of 1998 they were more or less forever at one another's sides.

When filming for *The Ninth Gate* began, Depp and Paradis had never properly met: by the time filming was complete, they were not just an item, but were expecting their first child. The tabloids tried to pin together stories that Depp and Moss had got back together, but the truth was that more than ever before in his life, Depp was truly settled with a partner.

With his domestic life on such a stable and happy footing at last, and with his fear of growing old without becoming a father allayed, there was much promise in the air for Depp when it came to his personal life. Professionally, though, he was not doing quite so well. In 1999, *The Astronaut's Wife* was released. This was a film about a NASA mission, in which Depp's supposedly heroic astronaut character turns out to be, in the words of the man who played him, 'just a full-on scumbag'. Although he appreciated the opportunity to debunk such a character, critical consensus was not favourable to the film, and neither were the box office takings.

The overall feeling with the film was that Depp was treading water; that his heart was not necessarily in the project – certainly not to the extent it was in previous cinematic outings. The American press noted cynically that the film house (New Line Cinema) had not even held press screenings. Once journalists finally got to see it, they were unimpressed, with the description 'ridiculously derivative' a typical reaction. On the back of the harsh critical reaction to *The Ninth Gate*, this was not a happy time for Depp to peruse write-ups of his work.

•

He needed a good project to bounce back with, one with the right director at the helm. Just such a project came his way in November 1998, in the shape of another film with Tim Burton: *Sleepy Hollow*. With Burton, Depp had previously produced pure cinema gold in the shape of *Ed Wood* and *Edward Scissorhands*. *Sleepy Hollow* was a period horror-cum-romance film, based on the Washington Irving story *The Legend of the Sleepy Hollow*. Depp was to play Ichabod Crane, a policeman sent to investigate a series of murders in a village, believed to have been committed by a headless horseman. During his investigation Crane falls in love with a woman, Katrina Van Tassel, played by Christina Ricci. 'Heads will roll', ran the chilling subtitle on the film's promotional posters.

For Depp it was a delight to reunite in a project with Burton, though part of the deal was that it would not be a simple task. 'Playing Ichabod was a great challenge,' he told the *Daily Express*. 'This is a character we grew up knowing very well, and of course I incorporated all the stuff from the book. But Paramount wouldn't let me wear a long nose and big ears.' He actually based his interpretation of the character on that given by Angela Lansbury's performance as Salome Otterbourne in the 1970s film *Death on the Nile*.

Filming took place in Britain, and Depp seemed to come alive once more as he tackled the part. No wonder, given that he was being directed by Burton, and starring alongside legendary British horror actor Christopher Lee. His decades-strong experience in cinema was a joy for Depp to observe and learn from as they performed. Lee was admiring of Depp, saying he did 'an excellent job' on the film.

The film's release was preceded by some ambitious online marketing, which helped build a sense of great anticipation. A 'family viewing' pressure group managed to help hype it still further when it criticized *Sleepy Hollow* for excessive goriness. Burton responded to their protests with inventiveness, remembering that when he was a child, 'I was probably more scared by seeing John Wayne or Barbra Streisand on the big screen than by seeing violence.'

The reviewers were delighted, too. Many singled out Depp for special praise, and several observed how well he performs when under Burton's direction.

Depp is often capable of surprising the world with his choices. Having been off-peak in his work for a short while, his return to form in *Sleepy Hollow* did not lead to him automatically seeking out more roles while he was hot again. Instead, he decided to step back and take a much-needed break. Having long insisted that he put his career second in life's priority list, he was good to his word. With a strong relationship with Paradis and a child on the way, there had never been a better time to step out of the breach. Having re-proved his abilities with *Sleepy Hollow*, he knew he would be able to return when the time suited him. 'I've been doing movies almost back-to-back since *Donnie Brasco*,' he explained. 'Now I'm taking it easy, spending time with my family.'

His first child, a daughter called Lily-Rose Melody Depp, was born on 27 May 1999. Depp was, he has always been proud to inform, present at the birth. 'I was there, yeah,' he said with a broad smile during a television interview with Charlie Rose. 'Unbelievable.' He has explained how it was both his mother, and Paradis's mother, who influenced his daughter's interesting name. 'In fact it was the only name that we'd come up with for a girl,' he said. 'We both loved the name "Lily", and I think her mom – Vanessa's mom – suggested the "Rose" part. Uhm . . . my mom's name is Betty-Sue and we wanted something that sounded kinda like Betty-Sue, that sort of southern thing. So "Lily-Rose". And "Melody", which is her middle name, was after a Serge Gainsbourg song called "Melody Nelson".'

He speaks with touching emotion and sincerity about becoming a father for the first time. For Depp, his life did not begin at forty, but rather, once he became a father. 'It's the only thing I've ever done. I mean it's the greatest thing I've ever done. It's amazing to finally meet the reason to live . . . your reason to live . . . ' He later went even further. 'Anything I've done up until 27 May 1999 was kind of an illusion, existing without living . . . The birth of my daughter gave me life,' he said.

His lifestyle changed in so many ways as a parent. For instance, he soon made a change to his drinking habits, which he found easier to do in his new life. 'I quit drinking spirits because I couldn't stop,' he said. 'I would just keep going until a black screen came down, where you can't see anything anymore. Trying to numb and medicate myself was never about recreation; it was existing without living. Now I have a solid foundation to stand on.'

Even in parenthood, he was sorely disappointed to discover, the media was as ruthless as ever in its pursuit of a valuable photograph to fill its pages and airtime with. When he was preparing to leave the hospital with his girlfriend and daughter, he was disgusted to see how many photographers were camped outside, poised to invade the privacy of such a tender and intimate moment for his family. 'There were about twenty-five paparazzi outside and it was like . . . I don't know – remora fish, you know? These blood suckers!' he said. 'I just couldn't believe it, that they would try to take something so sacred and so special . . . I mean, your first child born happens one time, obviously, and these people outside they are trying to turn it into some kind of a circus.'

There was to be no respite. When they finally arrived at Paradis's parents' home, they thought that at last they had found some quiet sanctuary. They breathed a sigh of relief, but with the next heartbeat they realized they were still under pursuit. 'Suddenly a helicopter swoops down above the yard and just hovered there for, like, ten minutes,' he remembered. 'We had to wait in the car until this thing left. I mean, that's bizarre. That's no way to live your life. That is no way to live your life.' Calling such media folk 'aggressive beasts', Depp attempted to empathize, but remained appalled. 'It's a greed thing,' he sniffed. 'I understand for some ... it's their bread-and-butter. OK, I'm with you on that. But an innocent, pure little child . . .'

He has later said that he finds media intrusions that focus on his children to be so infuriating that he feels 'beyond suing'. Instead, he said, 'I just wanted to beat whoever was responsible into the earth – I just wanted to rip him apart.'

On a more serene note, he also explained that becoming a father had given him a better perspective on life's irritations. Given how much the gossip and speculation of the press has got Depp down in the past, it was warming to learn that he was now able to put those pressures in their correct context. 'I would say that the kiddies give you strength – strength and perspective,' he said. 'Things that would've made me upset or angry before, or things about Hollywood, in magazines or paparazzi – stuff like that – now you can go, "Oh, piss off! I'm going to play Barbies with my daughter".'

With the increased joy came a rise in responsibility. He recalls a rising sense of paranoia engulfing him in his early days as a parent. 'I was nervous around the baby and every night I would sneak into the room where she was sleeping and put my hand in her crib, holding her little finger, and sleep on the floor next to her just to make sure she'd be all right,' he told the *News of the World*. 'I thought the warmth of my hand might help – that maybe if she felt my pulse it would remind her to breathe. I like kids and I've had plenty of practice as a babysitter,' he said. If this made it sound that he was taking fatherhood lightly, then other statements he has made have suggested quite the opposite. 'My sister Christine had a baby when I was seventeen and I was terrified about it because I had just read a long article about cot death. The most horrible thing was that the doctors had no idea what was causing babies to die, what made them stop breathing for no apparent reason.'

Here we have the first serious moments of adult domesticity for Johnny Depp, who had often lived like a teenage rebel into his twenties and thirties. He and Paradis moved into a new place in the south of France, and he quickly grew to love the life there. 'It's wonderful to be living in a tiny village with nothing around,' he said of the neighbourhood of the rural farmhouse they had purchased near St Tropez. It was, he added 'the simple life' that he so enjoyed, including visits to the local market. 'You can . . . do things they did one hundred and two hundred years ago.'

With a stable relationship with a woman and a child to care for, he felt a sense of completeness, tranquillity and clarity. 'Things are much clearer than they ever were,' he said with enthusiasm. 'The one thing that was missing in my life has now arrived.' He was even willing to roll his sleeves up and help out in the kitchen. 'I could never cook my entire life, I could never cook a thing,' he said of the years prior to this. 'Toast was a real stretch for me. Now suddenly I can cook. It's just ... I can cook stuff, like – not just like spaghetti and Ragu but, like – stuff.'

•

Refreshed and newly house-trained, he was ready to return to the cinematic fray. It had been a period of rest from work in which his life had changed dramatically. When he returned, he would soon take part in films that were more mainstream than most of those he had participated in to date. Still, though, he liked to think that he remained true to some basic principles. 'I don't have a deep strategy about which films I want to make,' he told the *News of the World*. 'But I refuse to do any movie that would make me want to throw up. That eliminates every dumb action movie, cop movie, or anything where people get blown up or shot every five minutes. I don't want to sound like some elitist who only does "serious" stuff – but I like to think I'm making films that actually say something about the world instead of simply trying to make a profit.' Before his next work proper, he had an honourable and proud engagement to fulfil.

In November 1999, he was awarded with his own star on the Hollywood Walk of Fame. 'It's certainly an incredibly great honour . . . being awarded with a star on Hollywood Boulevard – as Tim said – allows people to walk all over you,' said Depp. As well as not wishing to be boastful, the ambiguity of this statement shows that he has never been quite sure about Hollywood. Though later, once he had moved away from America, he did mellow slightly. 'The five years that I've been living in France have done wonders for my relationship with Hollywood,' he said. 'And also having kids . . . I'm so removed from it, I don't know anything. I don't know who anybody is, who's famous, who's rich, who's poor, who's successful, who's a drag. I don't know what made money or what didn't. It's great! I don't have to think about anything but my work.' How his life had improved since he and Kate Moss had parted ways.

Ms Moss, meanwhile, had not fared so well since the split. She checked into the famous Priory rehabilitation clinic to receive treatment for her alcohol issues, which, by her own admission had got 'a bit messy'. Given her recent relationship with Depp, the media could not resist the opportunity to relate her continuing story to her split with the film legend. Was she drinking so excessively to try and mend her broken heart? wondered some. Reports tried to prop up this theory by claiming that Depp had brought her a brand new BMW as some sort of guilt offering. However, there was no truth in this, said Moss, though she did insist that he had been most supportive. 'I was in love with him and I haven't been in love with anyone since,' she said. 'It was quite an intense relationship for four years and for a while there, it seemed kind of like it wasn't real. But it was.'

As the years went on, Moss, whose relationship with Depp had been so celebrated and discussed by the world, has had a roller coaster existence. She became a mother, but then became embroiled with controversial singer Pete Doherty. Drug scandals and outrage galore followed: at times she must have wished for the comparative serenity of life with Depp. He, however, always spoke positively of her, brushing aside the increasing controversy that the media showered upon her after their split. 'Dragging her through the mud like that – they are weird and two-faced. Let her be! I have never met Pete Doherty, but I think he has talent and he and Kate could be great together. She's got a great brain on her and she's a good mummy.'

●

Back in movieland, three films featuring Depp were released in 2000. The first was called *Before Night Falls*, directed by Julian Schnabel, who, said Depp, 'could not have been cooler about the whole thing'. It was based on the memoir of the rebellious Cuban artist Reinaldo Arenas, who died after battling AIDS. The film starred Javier Bardem, and Depp took two minor, cameo roles portraying contrasting characters: Lt Victor, a soldier, and a flamboyant transvestite named Bon Bon.

In terms of his standing among the cast, the roles were somewhat reversed for Depp. Just as Brando and Pacino had been the legends to him in his earlier films, this time it was *he* who was the legend of the line-up. Bardem enjoyed learning from him, describing Depp as, 'very generous, very helpful'. He made quite an impression on the lead, who concluded he admired him a great deal as 'an actor and a human being'.

Anyone seeing the promotional poster for his next film, *Chocolat*, might have thought Depp was the lead. Instead, his involvement was the same as that in *Before Night Falls* – a pair of minor, yet enjoyable, appearances.

The filming took place in England and France, so the set-up was especially convenient for him in his reiterated determination to spend more time with his family. He loved the film, which was directed by Lasse Hallström, his director from *What's Eating Gilbert Grape*. 'He's a great actor with great taste and classy choices,' said the director of Depp.

With this film Depp had chosen to play yet another outsider, a gypsy called Roux, who only appears after an hour has already passed in the movie. Given his ability and standing in the industry, it is to Depp's credit that he was willing to consider small roles in films that were never going to top the viewing charts. Indeed, for this one he was even stepping outside his culinary preferences, as someone who is not a big fan of chocolate.

Having finished his work on *Chocolat*, it was time for Depp to take his first lead role for a while. He assuaged fears that parenthood would sap him of his ambition by signing on to play notorious real-life drug dealer, George Jung, in the film *Blow*. Again, to prepare for filming Depp went the extra mile – in this case, by twice visiting Jung in prison.

Depp felt a few nerves as he showed up at the Otisville Federal Correctional Institute in New York, having sorted as best he could through the 'several thousand questions that swirled inside' his head.

On meeting Jung, he said the first three minutes of their encounter were awkward, but then it was as if they had known each other for 'a thousand years – or more'. Depp spoke admiringly of Jung later, describing how 'he was generous, he was gentle, he was hilarious, he was heartbreaking, he was all too human – a kind of outcast Zen Master who'd grabbed hold of life by the short and curlies and swung it around for all it was worth'. Memorably upbeat words, and it's true to say that Depp felt enormous sympathy for Jung. He has made clear that, but for a few different circumstances, he could easily have ended up living similarly to Jung.

Indeed, to connect with Jung, Depp found common standing between them. He recalled that he had entered the acting trade with an element of reluctance. His first dream had been for a career in music, but when he realized how much money could be made in the movies, he chose that path. He felt that Jung's path into the depths of drug dealing was similar. 'He was just following what looked at first like a promising future,' he said.

Blow's director, Ted Demme, had been present at the meetings between actor and convict. He noted the easy rapport they quickly established. 'I was amazed by the amount of philosophical things they agree upon. They both worship Bob Dylan (who would be featured on the soundtrack of *Blow*) and Jack Kerouac. It was fun watching them mould into one.'

As well as meeting Jung, Depp studied the facts of the drug-dealing world, to help him understand what might have motivated a seemingly humane man into entering it. He concluded that the need for an adrenaline rush was foremost.

Having studied Jung's mannerisms and quirks during a pair of quite intense and, naturally, limiting prison visits, Depp wondered if he could pull it off on set. He certainly could, as it turned out. 'He really got his body language,' said one of the crew, Georgia Kacandes, adding that Depp even started to look like Jung 'in a weird way'.

The producer, Joel Stillerman, was also impressed, saying it had been necessary for Depp to make the character more than just a drug dealer. In this challenge, Stillerman felt that Depp was more than successful. 'He brings a cerebral quality,' he purred.

Working at the head of a fine cast that included Penélope Cruz, Ray Liotta, Rachel Griffiths and Franka Potente, Depp was commanding as he stepped back into a leading role. As the BBC website wrote, 'Depp, an actor of terrific intelligence, insight and range, easily transforms himself from peppy youngster to sad, shambling failure'. *The Guardian*'s Peter Bradshaw was damning and bitchy, saying that Depp in character resembled 'a permanently hungover Francis Rossi lookalike in a [Status] Quo tribute band.'

Commercially, the film was a success, though it had a tragic postscript when its director, Demme, died not long after its release. Depp felt tormented with shock as he flew to America for the funeral of a man who was two years his junior.

Most significant to Depp was not the critical, nor the commercial, success of his films. He enjoyed both when they came, but as the world entered a new millennium, he was more pleased that his personal life was still such a happy affair. He had a wonderful, increasingly deep and rewarding relationship with Paradis, and together they had a beautiful daughter.

The twenty-first century would bring with it further happiness and success for him, both at work and at home. The profitable, mainstream movies he would take on brought him much satisfaction. Most joyful for him, though, was his growing domestic joy, which soared higher when Paradis gave birth to their second child.

CHAPTER SEVEN:

FAMILY MAN

At 1.30 a.m. on 9 April 2002, Depp became a father once more when Paradis gave birth to a baby boy. A spokeswoman for the couple said: 'Mother and son are doing great,' as the news broke around the world. Paradis and Depp named the boy Jack John Christopher Depp III.

In the aftermath of the birth the couple once more explained that they had no immediate plans to marry. It is interesting that after marrying once, and then becoming engaged twice, only to see those relationships falter, Depp was now content to live as husband and wife with his partner, but without formalizing the arrangement. His parents' marriage had failed, his own attempts at marriage/engagement had also not worked. Yet here he was enjoying a blissful bond with a woman he had no intention of marrying.

In 2001 he had jumped into a new film, called *From Hell*. In it he played a detective working in London during the nineteenth-century era of Jack the Ripper. His character was named Inspector Fred Abberline, and was an opium-user, bringing Depp his second drug-using character in a matter of a few years. Naturally, the Jack the Ripper connection captured Depp's imagination from the off, taking him back to those childhood days when he had obsessively read about the man and his reign of terror. Now he was being paid to once more immerse himself in this dark world. With a sense of dark delight he took a Jack the Ripper walking tour of London, which included a drink at The Ten Bells, the East End pub from whence many of the Ripper's victims were plucked.

The movie itself was filmed in a purpose-built set in Prague, which depicted a section of east London's Whitechapel. It was a three-month shoot but Paradis and Lily-Rose were in town, ensuring emotional continuity for the family.

The film was directed by two brothers: Allen and Albert Hughes. During one emotionally intense and sensitive scene, Allen felt that Depp could be acting it differently. In a directorial intervention that Depp would later describe as 'most beautiful', Allen leaned over and whispered into his ear, 'No sunshine'. The fact the actor appreciated his approach resonated with Allen, who found Depp to be 'the sweetest person on the planet'.

Released in 2001, the film was a hit, thanks in no small part to Depp's performance. 'Depp is very good as this decent, embattled man and his London accent is unobtrusive and quite as convincing as most British actors' American ones,' wrote the hard-to-please Observer.

Unbeknown to him, a leading part in the first instalment of what was going to become a blockbusting franchise was just around the corner for Depp. First, though, he had two lesser cinematic projects to engage in. He had been 'stupefied' by the script that was sent to him for a Terry Gilliam film called *The Man Who Killed Don Quixote*. Sadly, the film was never to be completed after being hit by a series of disasters that were, in the end, almost comical.

As the cast and crew arrived in the desert-like area of northern Spain for filming, torrential rain arrived and made the landscape entirely unsuitable for work. No sooner had the area become dry than it was earmarked by NATO for bombing practice. Then one of the movie's lead actors suffered from a double herniated disc and was forced to withdraw. Perhaps unsurprisingly, the project was then cancelled, which was a creative as well as a commercial disappointment for Depp.

Then, in 2002, he made a cameo appearance in the film *Lost in La Mancha*. Also during this highly productive time he directed a pair of promotional videos for Paradis's latest singles, 'Que Fait La Vie' and 'Pourtant'. He also made a brief appearance on stage during one of Paradis's concerts, playing guitar, having also contributed guitar tracks to some of her recent recordings.

In June 2002, Johnny arrived in England with Paradis and their two children at his side. The fact he was a parent was to prove crucial to his success as he played the part of J.M. Barrie, the author of *Peter Pan*, in the film *Finding Neverland*. Full of the innocent wonders of childhood as the parent of two young kids, he had, according to director Marc Forster, 'a beautiful sense about him, of . . . having this child within him alive'. Foster added that Depp was a natural in relating to children: 'He could fit right in there and play with them.'

As for Depp, who played alongside Kate Winslet, Julie Christie and child star Freddie Highmore, he too felt his newfound parenthood was the key that unlocked the performance. 'The idea behind *Neverland* is: from your imagination, make your dream life,' he told *Life* magazine in 2004. 'I don't have to close my eyes to see it because I live with it every day, with my kids, my girl and my life.' His connection with the character showed on screen – Depp was sensational.

As a parent, Depp now had two potential critics in his household. Obviously, many of the films he had appeared in were entirely inappropriate to be shown to viewers as young as his kids, so he was pleased to take part in a film more suitable to share with them. 'It's not like I'm going after any particular audience, but *Neverland* was great because it was much more accessible to my kids than, say, *Fear and Loathing*,' he told *Esquire*.

The cast and crew were very admiring, the director noting particularly a 'very special connection' between

Depp and Highmore. Winslet, meanwhile, reprised an observation that had already been made about him: 'Johnny almost isn't like an American at all. He's got such an English sense of humour.'

After the filming finished, Depp was on cloud nine. Speaking of his life, he said, 'It's as perfect as it could possibly be'. He was nominated in the Best Performance by an Actor in a Leading Role category of the Academy Awards and the equivalent category of the Golden Globes for his part. For *Neverland* he received some of the most lavish praise and applause of his career.

●

It was the aforementioned sense of childhood wonder, and his excitement at the thought of playing a part his kids would enjoy, that informed Depp's next, surprising move. Jerry Bruckheimer had big ambitions for the film he began making in the autumn of 2002. The man who had directed such works as *Flashdance*, *Beverly Hills Cop* and *Top Gun* had a huge budget of $125 million to create what he wanted to become the greatest pirate film of all time. It was set to be a mainstream blockbuster, but the director wanted a lead who could perform more than that; someone who could be 'darker, edgier'. He turned to Depp, who quickly agreed to take part in the film: *Pirates of the Caribbean: The Curse of the Black Pearl*. He was to play Captain Jack Sparrow, in a role that became one of the most iconic characters of twenty-first-century cinema to date.

His fellow cast members included Orlando Bloom, Keira Knightley and – playing Jack Sparrow's nemesis Captain Barbossa – Geoffrey Rush. Depp got to work. 'It was just a gas, it's probably the most centred and content I've ever been,' he said. However, in the first week of filming he found himself being nervously observed by the great and good of Walt Disney Pictures, who were anxious to see how Depp would play in a film they wanted to be both family and mainstream. Indeed, the tension continued more than a month into filming, with Depp being taken aside for 'chats'.

Thankfully, Depp had the confidence to stick by his own beliefs and instincts, and in the end the same executives were full of praise for his performance. He was graceful in his vindication, perhaps realizing that their apprehension has been well intentioned, and motivated, in part, because they had a hint of just how big the *Pirates* movie could become.

On its release in 2003, *Pirates of the Caribbean: The Curse of the Black Pearl* became very big indeed. It was the fourth highest grossing film of the year and earned Depp a nomination in the Actor in a Leading Role category at the Academy Awards, though he did not entirely enjoy the ceremony. 'All Vanessa and I could think was, when and where can we go smoke?' He won the MTV award for Best Performance.

Interestingly, he had based his interpretation of Captain Jack Sparrow on a curious combination: a Rastafarian, cartoon skunk hero Pepe Le Pew and Rolling Stones hellraiser Keith Richards, who later observed humorously that only now did he understand why Johnny had always been prepared to pay when they ate out together – he was obviously researching for the role!

All in all, Depp had found that his part in a commercial blockbuster had not come at the expense of enjoyment. 'Joy, mayhem, chaos,' he said when asked what the vital ingredients would be for a successful pirate film. There was enough of each to keep him smiling. His joy was infectious. 'There's no B.S., no attitude,' said director Gore Verbinski. 'He enjoys acting and it shows.'

Keira Knightley had been a little concerned before meeting Depp. She was only too aware of the stories about drink, drugs and a destroyed hotel room. 'You've read all these things,' she said. 'But he's such a nice bloke. He'd make a cup of tea, and we'd have a chat and giggle.'

By the time *Pirates* was hitting the screens, Depp had turned forty, a milestone in the life of any man. The first film of his fifth decade was *Secret Window*, based on a short novel written by Stephen King about a crazed reader who accuses an author – Depp's character Mort Rainey – of plagiarism. The film was directed by David Koepp, who reaffirmed the observation – previously made about Depp by Mike Newell, and indeed once made by Depp himself – about his lead actor being like 'a sponge'.

Explaining how Depp absorbs what is happening around him, Rainey said: 'Like that jaw thing he does . . . you've got to be careful what you do around him because he'll steal it from you.'

Johnny was on similar absorbing form when he filmed a brief cameo appearance in the 2004 French art house flick, *Happily Ever After*, alongside Charlotte Gainsbourg. This small involvement in a minority interest film was atypical of where Depp stood at this stage in his career. Having taken a step into the true blockbusting mainstream cinema world, he kept one foot in that heady sphere.

Two decades on from when he tried to shake off the 'sex symbol' status that he'd acquired, he was still a man who set hearts fluttering. *People* magazine's readers voted him the Sexiest Man Alive in 2004. It was a mixed year for him; he felt comfortable with the way he blended his leading roles in big commercial films such as *Pirates* and *Once Upon A Time in Mexico*, with cameo appearances in smaller flicks.

•

Meanwhile, he remained the devoted father to his two children, and a loving husband-in-all-but-name to Paradis. However, when Marlon Brando died in July 2004, Depp was devastated. He had lost an inspiration, a co-star and a friend. The following year Hunter S. Thompson also died, and the passing of these two friends – and legends – reminded Depp again of the value of leaving behind an impressive body of work.

To that end, he again joined forces with Tim Burton. The film would be another one to set the world alight, and appeal to his two children: thereby fulfilling the twin brief that was increasingly informing his choices. The new project would be a remake of that classic children's story *Willy Wonka and the Chocolate Factory*.

For a long time Depp had loved the stories of Roald Dahl, and when the director casually ran the idea for the film past him over dinner one evening, he agreed immediately to take the lead role. For Depp, memories flooded back of watching the original 1970s film of the story, starring Gene Wilder. 'Wilder's performance as Wonka was so definitive and seared into everyone's brains that I knew right away that I couldn't go anywhere near where he took the part,' he said, adding that Wilder had 'left a big pair of shoes to fill'. Indeed, his children had often watched the original 1970s film on

DVD, though Depp would 'run out of the room' when it came on, to avoid becoming influenced by Wilder's take on the character.

He prepared for this role by rehearsing the voice of his Wonka character in front of his daughter Lily-Rose, by now six years of age. 'It seemed to work with her so I kind of ran with it,' he said.

Choosing to base his interpretation of Wonka on 'a kind of game-show host-cum-bratty child', Depp was masterful in the film. 'Johnny Depp's deliciously demented take on Willy Wonka, the candyman of Roald Dahl's book, demands to be seen,' said *Rolling Stone* magazine, speaking for many critics and indeed everyday viewers. Taking $206,466,43 at the box office, this was the second most profitable film (after *Pirates*) that Depp had taken part in up until now. But even this film's takings would soon be dwarfed by future Depp movies.

However Johnny's part in *Willy Wonka* – and the voice parts he was simultaneously recording for Burton's fantasy animation *Corpse Bride* – came with a price. As he worked in England, he felt very homesick and missed Paradis and their children who were back in France. He flew home most Friday evenings, only to return to England on the Sunday, ready to start work again. When he committed to film two more instalments of the *Pirates* series, he did so with a vow that his work on them would interrupt his family life no more than was necessary.

He was delighted to be able to revisit his Captain Jack Sparrow character, saying he had always held a 'sneaking suspicion' that there would be more opportunities to portray him in the future and that he always felt 'an odd kind of depression' at the end of a film, when he had to leave a character behind. Filming for part two of the *Pirates* series – *Dead Man's Chest* – would be immediately followed by the shooting of part three – *At World's End* –giving the star a good run of time portraying Sparrow on set in the Bahamas.

Dead Man's Chest opened in July 2006, and any fears that it would not equal the success of its predecessor were washed away when it took $135 million in its first weekend in America. It went on to surpass the takings of the first instalment, as the world fell in love with the *Pirates* series, not least the presence of Depp so brilliantly leading the story. It felt, at times, a little convoluted in its plot, but the *Pirates'* magic was there again in abundance, with the characters having pleasantly grown since the first movie.

'Wall-to-wall fun,' wrote the *Daily Mail*'s Baz Bamigboye. Depp was the focal point of many critics' praise, though he declared himself 'shocked' by the way his character had so firmly grabbed people's imagination. It would do that once again when the third *Pirates* movie was released in May 2007.

By the time he began work on the third *Pirates* chapter,

he had followed in the footsteps – or perhaps that should be 'handsteps' – of many a Hollywood legend by leaving his handprints on the pavement outside Mann's Chinese Theatre in Los Angeles. This, quite literally, cemented his place in the movieland elite.

In *At World's End*, Depp was joined by yet another of his heroes, and the man who had partially informed his interpretation of Captain Jack Sparrow, Rolling Stone Keith Richards. 'God, it was great,' he said of working alongside Richards. He spoke with understandable wonder at how Richards would arrive 'totally prepared, like beautiful' for work at half past seven in the morning. So quickly did Richards nail his scenes that Depp took to nicknaming him 'Two-Take Richards'.

On its release, the BBC's was one of several very negative reviews of the film, saying it 'clunks like a rusty anchor'. But in truth this was not the sort of film that critics felt inclined to view favourably – commercial ventures rarely are. Commercial indeed it was, taking a record $401 million in the first six days of its release. The audience loved it and it was another piece of work that Depp could share with his children. He admitted that he was sad at the end of filming.

With no further films in the series confirmed at that stage, it felt like the end of an enjoyable era for Depp. He cried as he wondered whether he was waving goodbye to Captain Jack Sparrow for good. 'I'll always hold him in very high regard,' said Depp of his beloved pirate hero, not realizing he would get yet another chance to play him. He did his best to encourage such a development, saying, 'I've never really felt I'm done with the character, so why shouldn't I try a fourth and a fifth?'

•

In the meantime, though, he had further business with his old pal Tim Burton to attend to in the shape of the film *Sweeney Todd*. Based on the famous musical of a murdering London barber, the film brought together his current career (acting) with his original dream (singing). The story is one of classic revenge, with Todd killing out of anger at his wrongful imprisonment and the problems that came his way as a result.

In connecting with the soul of the man he portrayed in the film, Depp openly expressed a sense of empathy. 'I think we all secretly have that feeling in us, but don't like to admit it,' he said. 'I'm a big fan of revenge!' He was not such a big fan of singing, though. During his time in bands he had kept vocal contributions to a minimum and in *Cry Baby*, the only other musical he had been in, his vocal parts were dubbed.

'There was definite trepidation,' he said, remembering his feelings about this. 'I didn't know if it was possible. I knew I wouldn't be tone deaf but I wasn't sure I could carry a song, let alone several, and something as complex as Stephen Sondheim's. It was real scary for both of us. And talk about the opportunity to really flop. It was one of those, "Let's turn the heat up a little".' Indeed, so shy was he about singing that he was even too 'mortified' to sing in the shower. He turned to Bruce Witkin, the bassist from his old band The Kids, for advice. Witkin flushed his old pal full of confidence, and honed the cockney delivery his character's vocals would need. The resulting confidence was clear on screen during *Sweeney Todd*, in which Depp acted and, yes, sang beautifully.

The film earned four Golden Globe nominations, including Best Performance by an Actor in a Motion Picture (Musical or Comedy) for Depp. He was also nominated for an Oscar, though he did not win that gong. He won in his Golden Globe category, but due to an industrial dispute, the awards were not handed out at the usual glittering, backslapping gala, but during a low-key press conference. For Depp, never a fan of awards ceremonies, this was probably the best way to receive such a prestigious award.

Burton was thrilled with Depp. He had a special fondness for some of his favourite actor's past roles – including Edward Scissorhands and Ed Wood – and Sweeney Todd was up there competing with those for the honour of his favourite Depp role. 'There were moments', Depp recalled, 'when Tim [Burton] said, "You know, I think this is my favourite character".' Burton took up this theme: 'I said to Johnny, if I was an actor, I swear to God, this would be the role I would love to play because you don't have to talk, you just stand there, staring out the window. Perfect.'

•

When Michael Mann approached Depp to appear in his film *Public Enemies*, about the Depression-era bank robber John Dillinger, he felt he was setting Depp a big challenge. 'What I was after,' he explained, 'was something I hadn't seen him do for a long time – play a tough man.' As we have seen, Depp has an imaginative and adaptable mind, one that can explore a character, and return with a common thread. The fact that he and Dillinger had come from the same part of America was one, albeit superficial, similarity they shared. He also looked to his own grandfather, who had 'run moonshine into dry counties . . .' and his stepfather who had also 'been a bit of a rogue and done burglaries and robberies and spent some time in Statesville Prison in Illinois, where we ended up shooting some of the film. There was some kind of inherent connection I had.' Again, therefore, Depp had sympathy for a devil. The fact the film was also set in an era that Depp had a lot of affection for – 'men were still elegantly dressed' – just sealed the appeal for him.

'John Dillinger was that era's rock and roll star,' Depp told *The Telegraph*. 'He was a very charismatic man and he lived the way he wanted to and didn't compromise. I feel he was a kind of Robin Hood because he truly cared about people. He knew time was short and I believe he had found himself and was at peace with the fact that it wasn't going to be a very long ride, but it was going to be a significant ride.' Say what you will about Depp, but his assessment of rogues such as Dillinger and Sweeney Todd is to be respected, if not universally admired.

When challenged on how he could so admire Dillinger, he pointed out that many people have broken the law in their lives. 'When I was twelve I wanted to learn how to play the guitar and I found a chord book in a shop and I stuffed it down my trousers,' he said.

While filming *Public Enemies* in locations across America, Depp took a break to play an unconventional role in a new Terry Gilliam film, *The Imaginarium of Doctor Parnassus*. Gilliam's project had been struck by a tragedy when its lead star, the young and talented Heath Ledger, died of an accidental drug overdose. The film seemed doomed to be scrapped, until Gilliam decided to complete it using a combination of actors to fill the remaining parts of Ledger's character. Depp, Jude Law and Colin Farrell all stepped up to the plate, and filming recommenced, and Depp donated his fee for the film to a trust fund set up for Ledger's daughter.

Of the three late stand-ins, Depp slipped into the role most gracefully and with least effort. Indeed, it was hard watching his scenes to remember that it was not the late Ledger. 'When Johnny appears, so many people think it's Heath,' said Gilliam. Both *Public Enemies* and *The Imaginarium of Doctor Parnassus* were cinema hits.

Having worked with little respite for some time, Depp took a much-deserved break at this stage. However, even during rest times, Depp's creative juices continued to flow. He directed another promotional video for a single Paradis had recorded and she and their two children were in the audience for one of the two shows he performed with his old band The Kids. 'Music will always be my first love,' he told *Rolling Stone* magazine.

Refreshed and relaxed, he was energized once again, ready to appear for the seventh time in a film for his favourite director, Tim Burton. This would be his first time in a 3D film, playing the Mad Hatter in Burton's new version of the classic tale *Alice in Wonderland*. Depp was wondrous as the Mad Hatter, though he was so heavily made up for the part, it was easy to forget it was him on screen. The loudness of his appearance in the film was the legacy of some pre-filming brainstorming sessions he and Burton had enjoyed, in which they painted watercolour sketches of how they imagined his character to look. Depp's painting made the character look, in his own words, 'like a weird clown', and so did the on-screen version, to a large extent.

Although it was to bring in over a billion dollars at the box office, *Alice in Wonderland* garnered mixed reviews from the critics. *Variety* magazine praised it for its 'moments of delight, humour and bedazzlement', while the *Los Angeles Times* said disparagingly, 'One pill makes you larger, one pill makes you small, and the pills Tim Burton gives you don't do very much at all'.

With a string of successful films in recent times, Depp was probably due a bit of a stinker. In many people's view, *The Tourist* was just that. During his headline-grabbing anchoring of the 2011 Golden Globes ceremony, Ricky Gervais took aim at the film saying: 'I haven't even seen *The Tourist*,' adding with a cheeky grin, 'Who has?'

In this thriller, directed by Florian Henckel von Donnersmarck, Depp plays opposite Angelina Jolie as an American tourist in Italy, led astray by Jolie. Curiously, despite his long-standing and strong friendship with her partner, Brad Pitt, Depp and Jolie had never previously met. 'We met oddly right before we did this which is weird because I think we have a lot of mutual friends and mutual acquaintances, people that we've worked with, however we'd never met. When we sat down together it was kind of instant. We got each other. Within minutes we were yakking about our kids and the perils of parenthood and all of that fun stuff. She's impressive. She's a force.' Between them, they constituted a potent leading partnership for the film, or as *The Independent* put it, '[the] collective star wattage is of supernova proportions'.

Perhaps unsurprisingly, Depp very much enjoyed shooting the more romantic scenes with the glamorous Jolie, but was quick to also deliver praise for her as a talent and a thinker. 'Yeah, I mean, I've had more difficult days at work, definitely,' said Depp of the love scenes. 'But those kinds of things are always awkward. So you just laugh your way through, and you just kind of giggle and feel stupid. But then Angelina is a kind of a walking poem – the perfect beauty who at the same time is very deep and very smart.'

With him and Jolie hitting it off on and off screen, her family and his would get together sometimes after filming. 'One night Angie and Brad came for dinner,' he said. 'They brought their son Pax and he played video games with my boy, Jack. They had a blast.' Jolie was just as complimentary in return. 'He was cooler and even more interesting than I'd imagined,' she said of Depp. 'I've seen him with his family; he is a great family man, a funny, lovely person who is gracious to people. A real Renaissance man.'

She was tickled by Depp's description of her and Pitt as the Richard Burton and Elizabeth Taylor of the twenty-first century. 'It's such a funny thing for Johnny to say,' she said. 'I take that as a very high compliment. I think he and his wife are such an extraordinary couple that I can't even imagine a comparison. You pretty much get a sense that this person [Depp] must have a good sense of humour and a good heart because all his characters seem to have a sensitive side and sense of fun, but you just never know until you meet somebody.'

Depp is no stranger to the pressures of fame, but even he confessed to being surprised when he witnessed the 'Brangelina' phenomena at first hand. 'I got a taste of it when we were making the film together, because it's very rare that you leave your hotel to go into a boat to go to work and you find yourself asking the guy out front, "How many are out there today?", and he says, "Oh there's thirty of them, in boats . . .",' he said. 'But Angie and Brad handle it so beautifully, and with such dignity and class. I don't think I'm capable of controlling myself to that degree.'

The two couples had so much in common. Both consisted of two famous partners, who had faced and continued to face the highs and lows of life in the public eye. Also, in both cases they had been together for many years but had yet to get married. In Depp's case, he had, by then, been with Paradis for twelve years, so it was natural that people would wonder whether they would ever tie the knot. 'If Vanessa wanted to get hitched, why not?' he replied when asked this by the *Mirror*. 'But the thing is I would be so scared of ruining her last name. She's got such a good last name.'

He went on to praise more than just her surname, lauding the positive effect she had had on his life. 'I was more at war with myself then,' he said of his life before they met. 'It took me a while to figure out what I wanted and then I met the woman who made me see what I was missing. But raising a family and spending so much time with our kids is what has really had the most calming influence on me. They became my focus and it put things into perspective. Nothing makes me happier than watching Vanessa and my kids and just realizing that they're my world. It's pure joy.'

With such domestic happiness, Depp is in a very good place as he approaches his fifties. It seems strange to consider a man who came to prominence as a teen pin-up reaching such an age. However, he has matured gracefully and with his good looks and charisma remains a man who can set the pulses of people – young and old – racing.

•

As he looks to the future, Depp can rest assured that he remains at the top of the tree. In 2010, the much-respected People's Choice Awards voted him Actor of the Decade. Often, when an actor has landed such a prestigious gong they face a backlash of exclusion in subsequent years. However, when the People's Choice Awards came around again in 2011, Depp was once more basking in glory. The glittering event, hosted by Queen Latifah in Los Angeles, saw nearly 200 million votes cast for the various categories – and Depp won the 2011 Favourite Movie Actor Award for his roles in *Alice in Wonderland* and *The Tourist*. He received a standing ovation as he accepted the prize. Depp has often insisted he is not motivated by a desire or need for awards. He does not often attend such ceremonies and has expressed discomfort when he has done so.

Actress Taylor Swift presented the award to Depp, who informed her, to her delight, that his daughter is a big fan. He thanked the audience and voters for the award, which he described as 'a stupefying honour'.

A more tangible honour came with the news that he had been named the top movieland earner for 2010. This was the third successive time he had landed at the top of this tree, and the fact that the runner-up was his *Tourist* co-star, Angelina Jolie, proved that despite the film's modest showing, both stars remained serious audience-drawers and revenue-generators for the industry. He also knocked the *Twilight* sensation Robert Pattinson off the top spot of the Internet Movie Database's Starmeter Top Twenty-five, in which the places are calculated by how many Internet searches are made for each star.

The surge in success and popularity Depp has enjoyed in the twenty-first century has not come at the expense of his comfort or principles. He continues to choose carefully what roles to take and has turned down many that may have provided an easy buck.

Not that he is in any way uptight or pretentious in his choosiness. For instance, one of his most recent films was a voice in the animated CGI comedy *Rango*. He provided the voice for the title character, in a film that also featured the voices of stars including Bill Nighy, Isla Fisher and Abigail Breslin. 'I think it just gives a bunch of grown-ups an opportunity to be silly,' he laughed. 'Rango is a lizard attempting to adapt to his surroundings,' he told *Entertainment Tonight*. 'He's trying to figure out what he's supposed to be, like most of us in life. It's certainly like nothing I've ever done before, or any of us have ever done before.'

Rango was directed by *Pirates* director Gore Verbinski, who took a characteristically novel approach to the making of the animated flick, eschewing the usual method of recording voices in studio booths, and instead getting his voice cast to act out the parts on a stage. 'It was just like rehearsing a high school play,' said Verbinski. 'Why give up on what we do in live action?'

In the same month, Depp explained that, for him, the chance to play eccentric, extravagant characters is preferable to playing more commonplace, everyday types. 'I like going back to [Captain Jack] and seeing what we can cook up. It's tougher to play someone like my character in *The Tourist*. I have the most fun when I can hide behind wigs or hats or make-up.'

When a fourth instalment of the *Pirates* franchise was announced, he was as overjoyed as the fans. He had a spring in his step as he returned to work on that series. During filming he had a spot of fun with a young fan. A nine-year-old British schoolgirl called Beatrice Delap, on hearing that Depp was filming at the eighteenth-century naval college near to her school in south-east London, decided to write to him with some mischief in mind. 'Dear Captain Jack Sparrow,' began her note. 'At Meridian Primary School, we are a bunch of budding young pirates and we were having a bit of trouble mutiny-ing against the teachers, and we'd love if you could come and help. Beatrice Delap, aged nine, a budding pirate. PS We have a plentiful supply of rum.'

To the delight of young Delap, Depp decided to visit the school. Giving the establishment ten minutes' notice of his impending arrival, Depp swept dramatically through the gates in a car with blacked-out windows. When he appeared in front of the children dressed in full pirate costume, Depp prompted what were described as 'incredible screams of joy'. Standing next to Delap, he showed her the letter she had sent him and then made her day by embracing her. 'He gave me a hug and he said, "Maybe we shouldn't mutiny today 'cos there are police outside monitoring me",' recalled the girl later.

This was not the first time that Depp had delighted London youngsters with an impromptu visit. The other episode was sparked by a near tragedy that had occurred in Depp's life in 2007. Depp and his family were staying in a rented mansion in Richmond, Surrey, while he filmed *Sweeney Todd* at Pinewood Studios in Buckinghamshire. While they were there, Lily-Rose became unwell, having caught a nasty bout of E. coli poisoning.

As her condition worsened, Depp was, naturally, beside himself with concern about his daughter, spending as much time as possible by her side and requiring regular updates about her condition while filming. As her state worsened so much that she was taken to hospital, he quit filming and rushed to her bedside at Great Ormond Street Hospital.

He later looked back at his terror during the uncertain hours, which was followed by enormous relief and gratitude when Lily-Rose returned to health, thanks to the medical staff at Great Ormond Street. 'It was the most frightening thing we have ever been through,' he said. 'It was hell. But the magic is that she pulled through beautifully. Great Ormond Street was terrific, a great hospital.'

The following January he and the film-makers put their money where their mouths were and donated huge sums to Great Ormond Street. Depp donated £1 million out of his own pocket; Walt Disney Pictures, the makers of the *Pirates* franchise, pledged to donate another £10 million themselves. These donations were especially welcomed by the hospital, as it had issued an appeal for £170 million required for its re-development plans. Depp's display of gratitude did not end there. He invited five Great Ormond Street doctors and nurses to the after-party that followed the London premiere of *Sweeney Todd*. Just a few months before all this he also spent four hours at the hospital reading stories for the sick and recovering children there.

As the world waited for the fourth instalment of the *Pirates* series to be released, Depp promised it would be easier to understand than the previous episodes. 'The thing with *Pirates 4*, I felt like we owed it to people to entertain them,' he told *Empire* magazine. '*Pirates* 2 and 3 became quite . . . sub-plotty. The mathematics of it. All these people went to see them two or three times just to figure out what was happening.' He continued: 'This one is a little closer in tone to the first, more character driven . . . more subject driven. It has a freshness and less mathematics.'

His co-star, Penélope Cruz, enjoyed working alongside Depp. She said his easy way with humour brought with it complications, though. 'Johnny is such a funny person, he has created this amazing character,' said Cruz. 'The main problem is that he's so funny it was hard to film the dramatic scenes, because I could not stop laughing. You never know what will happen next.'

What *will* happen next for Johnny Depp? As we have seen, he has many skills and ambitions, and it pays to expect the unexpected from him. He has his eyes set on tackling Shakespeare on stage. '*Hamlet* is one of those actor cliché things that bounces around in your head,' he said. 'Many years ago, Marlon Brando planted that seed in my skull and said, "Kid, you really should play *Hamlet* before you get too long in the tooth". He never got to play it, and so he kept hammering me to just take off, forget movies, and go do it. And so I've thought about it more and more lately; the thing I'd like to do with *Hamlet* is to do it as under the radar as possible, in a very tiny theatre, and if it caught on then you could just move it somewhere else, to a rec [recreational] hall somewhere.'

As well as dreaming of appearing in *Hamlet*, Depp and his family spend an increasing amount of time living in a hamlet. 'We have a great little place in the south of France,' he explained. 'It's a little hamlet – only about forty-five acres.' How blissful – one should not expect him and his family to return to America any time soon. He watches the news reports of increasingly violent goings-on in the States with concern. 'You see little kids going into schools and shooting each other up. I mean, that is no longer a rare occurrence over there. And that's madness. I don't want to live with that. I don't want my daughter or my son to grow up watching that kind of thing on TV. If I have my way, they would never know there was such a thing as bad or evil. They would believe everyone is good.'

Touching and sensitive sentiments from a man who is a wonderful, modern father. Modern in emotions, but not technologically. For him one of the appeals of where he lives is that it gives him a chance to avoid the ever-present influence of technology elsewhere. 'Sometimes I'd like to run away screaming from our technology-obsessed world, the invasive media, the madness of reality TV,' he said. 'We've lost touch with the simple things of life. We're losing our individuality.'

Therefore, he argued, having his own island, Little Hall's Pond Cay in the Bahamas, was a natural extension to this yearning he feels for a closer connection with nature. 'The island might sound extravagant but I need somewhere I can breathe easily or just sit around and chat without someone taking my picture,' he explained. 'It provides me with simplicity and somewhere I can go, where no one is looking at me or pointing a camera or finger at me.' He went on to explain that while on the island he and his family did very little – and that was the point of it. 'I can just be; that's the importance of it. When we're there we do absolutely nothing. My kiddies don't have any toys there and they build little houses out of shells.' Sometimes, he has spent up to three months at a time in this blissfully simple existence. 'I literally just wake up, go out, check the garden and see the vegetables growing. It's a pristine existence in terms of simplicity. There's no talk of movies or work and, infinitely more important, the telephone never rings.'

Will he and Paradis ever marry? If they do, it will surely be a quiet, modest arrangement. Even if they do not marry, they live to all intents and purposes as man and wife. He looks set to be with her for good. 'Well, when I see a couple celebrating their seventy-fifth wedding anniversary, I just think that it's totally incredible,' he once said, when asked whether he ever got 'mushy'. 'Or when I see someone who just follows their dream and succeeds, and just does basically what they want to do and doesn't have to answer to anyone – obviously not harming anyone – that's great.'

POSTSCRIPT

His has been an extraordinary, admirable existence. When he looks back over his life to date, Johnny Depp has few regrets. 'There were the things that I probably should have done,' he told legendary American television interviewer Charlie Rose. 'Not from my perspective. I mean, from my point of view I did the right things. Every film that I've done, I'm happy that I made that choice. I don't have any regrets whatsoever. But I mean in terms of sustaining box-office bankability, I should have done a few of the things that I didn't do. But I'm glad I didn't do them.'

With the riches he has earned, not least from the *Pirates* series and some of his other recent blockbusters, were Depp never to work again, he could keep himself and his family comfortable for the rest of their lives. However, despite occasionally joking about his plans, he has no intention of stopping acting anytime soon. 'I think I'll act until I make enough money to buy my own planet and move onto it. Uh, no, as long as I can keep doing stuff that I want to do and have fun, then I'll be doing it.'

He looks forward to the day when he can look back. He imagines himself sitting by a lake, looking out at the water, with a fine old beer belly under his shirt. As long as he deserves the respect of his grandchildren, he will feel he has done well. It would be hard for his grandchildren to not respect him, as millions of fans do across the planet. When he looks beyond his retirement, he hopes to be remembered as a talent who was always 'alive'. For his epitaph, this man, for whom music was always a bigger love than acting, would choose two sets of lyrics from a song by blues legend Bessie Smith. 'Gimme a pigfoot and a bottle of beer. Send me 'gain. I don't care,' and, 'Gimme me a reefer and a gang o' gin. Slay me 'cause I'm in my sin'.

Hardly the most conventional of epitaphs, but then that's Johnny Depp for you.

PICTURE CREDITS AND BIBLIOGRAPHY

PICTURE CREDITS

Page 1: © Tristar / Everett / Rex Features

Page 2: Everett Collection / Rex Features (above); Lester Cohen / WireImage / Getty Images (below)

Page 3: Splash News (above left); © Globe Photos / Alpha (above right); Sipa Press / Rex Features (below left); Kevin Mazur / WireImage / Getty Images (below right)

Page 4: © 20th Century Fox / Everett / Rex Features

Page 5: Everett Collection / Rex Features (both)

Page 6: Tim Rooke / Rex Features (above left); Rex Features (above right); Alex Berliner / BEI / Rex Features (below)

Page 7: © Christophe d'Yvoire / Sygma / Corbis (above); Brian Rasic / Rex Features (below)

Page 8: SNAP / Rex Features

Page 9: Sipa Press / Rex Features (above); Sutton-Hibbert / Rex Features (below left); Joyce Silverstein / Rex Features (below right)

Page 10: Rex Features (above left & right); Alex Berliner / BEI / Rex Features (below)

Page 11: Getty Images (above); Dave Lewis / Rex Features (centre); WENN (below)

Page 12: Kore Press / Rex Features (above left); Everett Collection / Rex Features (above right); © 20th Century Fox / Everett / Rex Features (below)

Page 13: © W. Disney / Everett / Rex Features

Page 14: © W. Disney / Everett / Rex Features (above); © BuenaVista / Everett / Rex Features (below)

Page 15: © Warner Bros / Everett / Rex Features (above); Everett Collection / Rex Features (below)

Page 16: Startraks Photo / Rex Features (above); © Col Pics / Everett / Rex Features (below)

BIBLIOGRAPHY

Johnny Depp: The Illustrated Biography, Nick Johnstone, Carlton Books, 2010

The Secret World of Johnny Depp, Nigel Goodall, John Blake Publishing, 2007

Depp, Christopher Heard, ECW Press, 2001

Johnny Depp: A Modern Rebel, Brain J. Robb, Plexus Publishing, 1995

INDEX

INDEX

INDEX

INDEX

INDEX